Conversational Arabic Dialogues

50 Arabic Conversations to Easily Improve Your Vocabulary & Become Fluent Faster

Conversational Arabic Dual Language Books Vol. 1

Touri
https://touri.co/

ISBN: 978-1-953149-22-0

Second Paperback Edition: July 2020
First Paperback Edition: March 2019

CONTENTS

FREE AUDIOBOOKS 1

Resources 2

Want the next Arabic book for free? 5

Introduction 6

Survival Phrases 10

1. تحية رسمية – Formal Introduction 17

2. تحية غير رسمية - Informal Greeting 19

3. مكالمة هاتفية – A Telephone Call 21

4. كم الساعة الان؟ – WHAT TIME IS IT? 23

5. هل يمكنك قول ذلك مجددًا؟ – Can You Say That Again? 25

6. مصادفات – Coincidences 27

7. الطقس – The Weather 29

8. طلب الطعام – Ordering Food 31

9. موعد مع الطبيب – Visiting The Doctor 33

10. السؤال عن الاتجاهات – Asking For Directions 35

11. طلب المساعدة – Calling For Help 37

12. التسوق – Shopping 39

13. إدارة المهمات – Running Errands 41

14. في مكتب البريد – At The Post Office 43

15. الامتحان – THE EXAM 45

16. السترة المثالية – THE PERFECT SWEATER 47

17. سيارة أجرة أم حافلة – TAXI OR BUS 49

18. كم تبلغ من العمر؟ – HOW OLD ARE YOU? 51

19. في المسرح – AT THE THEATER 53

20. ما هي الأشياء التي أنت جيد في القيام بها؟ – WHAT ARE YOU GOOD AT DOING?.55

21. ما هي الرياضة المفضلة لديك؟ – WHAT IS YOUR FAVORITE SPORT? 57
22. الذهاب لمشاهدة مسرحية موسيقية – GOING TO SEE A MUSICAL..............................59
23. أخذ إجازة – Taking A Vacation...61
24. في متجر الحيوانات – At The Pet Store 63
25. التعبير عن رأيك – EXPRESSING YOUR OPINION...65
26. الهوايات – HOBBIES 67
27. حفلة الزواج – THE WEDDING 69
28. تقديم النصيحة – GIVING ADVICE 71
29. تعليم الاطفال – TEACHING CHILDREN...73
30. متعة لعب كرة المضرب – FUN WITH TENNIS 76
31. العيش في كاليفورنيا – LIVING IN CALIFORNIA..79
32. الطهي – BAKING..83
33. مساعدة عبر الهاتف – HELP OVER THE PHONE..86
34. هيّا نذهب إلى حفلة موسيقية – LET'S GO TO A CONCERT......................................90
35. القيام بخطط – MAKING PLANS 93
36. العطلة الشتوية – WINTER BREAK 96
37. زيارة الطبيب – VISITING THE DOCTOR...99
38. السوق – THE MARKET 103
39. دعنا نحصل على شقة – LET'S GET AN APARTMENT 106
40. موقف الامتياز – THE CONCESSSION STAND 109
41. وقت الغداء – LUNCHTIME 112
42. البحث عن وظيفة – SEARCHING FOR A JOB..115
43. مقابلة الوظيفة – JOB INTERVIEW..118
44. تقديم عرض – GIVING A PRESENTATION 122
45. التخرج – GRADUATION...125
46. الهالوين – HALLOWEEN...127
47. في فندق – AT A HOTEL 130
48. طالبة أجنبية – A FOREIGN STUDENT 133

FREE AUDIOBOOKS

RESOURCES

TOURI.CO

Some of the best ways to become fluent in a new language is through repetition, memorization and conversation. If you'd like to practice your newly learned vocabulary, Touri offers live fun and immersive 1-on-1 online language lessons with native instructors at nearly anytime of the day. For more information go to Touri.co now.

FACEBOOK GROUP

Learn Spanish - Touri Language Learning

Learn French - Touri Language Learning

YOUTUBE

Touri Language Learning Channel

ANDROID APP

Learn Spanish App for Beginners

BOOKS

SPANISH

Conversational Spanish Dialogues: 50 Spanish Conversations and Short Stories

Spanish Short Stories (Volume 1): 10 Exciting Short Stories to Easily Learn Spanish & Improve Your Vocabulary

Spanish Short Stories (Volume 2): 10 Exciting Short Stories to Easily Learn Spanish & Improve Your Vocabulary

Intermediate Spanish Short Stories (Volume 1): 10 Amazing Short Tales to Learn Spanish & Quickly Grow Your Vocabulary the Fun Way!

Intermediate Spanish Short Stories (Volume 2): 10 Amazing Short Tales to Learn Spanish & Quickly Grow Your Vocabulary the Fun Way!

100 Days of Real World Spanish: Useful Words & Phrases for All Levels to Help You Become Fluent Faster

100 Day Medical Spanish Challenge: Daily List of Relevant Medical Spanish Words & Phrases to Help You Become Fluent

FRENCH

Conversational French Dialogues: 50 French Conversations and Short Stories

French Short Stories for Beginners (Volume 1): 10 Exciting Short Stories to Easily Learn French & Improve Your Vocabulary

French Short Stories for Beginners (Volume 2): 10 Exciting Short Stories to Easily Learn French & Improve Your Vocabulary

Intermediate French Short Stories (Volume 1): 10 Amazing Short Tales to Learn French & Quickly Grow Your Vocabulary the Fun Way!

ITALIAN

Conversational Italian Dialogues: 50 Italian Conversations and Short Stories

GERMAN

Conversational German Dialogues: 50 German Conversations and Short Stories

RUSSIAN

Conversational Russian Dialogues: 50 Russian Conversations and Short Stories

CHINESE

Conversational Chinese Dialogues: 50 Chinese Conversations and Short Stories

WANT THE NEXT ARABIC BOOK FOR FREE?

https://touri.co/premium-access-arabic-dialogues/

INTRODUCTION

So you're ready to take the plunge and learn Arabic? What an excellent choice you have made to expand your horizons and open more doors to opportunities in your life.

If this is your first time or a continuation of your Arabic learning journey, we want you to know that we're proud of you.

Arabic is the primary language of the Arab World mostly found in Asia, Middle East, and North Africa. Approximately 420 million speak Arabic which makes it the fifth most popular language in the world. Did you know that Arabic is derived from the word Arab referring to the Bedouins since Arabic originated from the Arabian Peninsula. This is a region which consists mainly of nomadic tribes.

You'll find there are many differences between Arabic and English, the most notable being that it is written from right to left. There are also a few sounds that don't exist in other languages, such as 'ح' , which is a 'h' sound as in 'hubb' (love). To get an idea of how this is pronounced, imagine breathing on a window pane to create a mist.

The ability to communicate in a foreign language will allow you to truly immerse yourself in different cultures, create even more memorable travel experiences and become more marketable for career opportunities.

It is human nature to naturally progress and learn from the day we are born. Since birth we have been shaping our preferences based on our previous experiences. These experiences have provided you important feedback about your likes, dislikes, what has made you better or worse and allowed you to learn from these lessons.

The same process should be taken to learn a language.

Our goal with this book is to provide engaging and fun learning material that is relevant and useful in the real Arabic-speaking world. Some students are provided with difficult or boring language materials that cause the learner to become overwhelmed and give up shortly after.

Building a strong foundation of vocabulary is critical to your improvement and reaching fluency. We *guarantee* you that this book is packed with vocabulary and phrases that you can start using today.

WHAT THIS BOOK IS ABOUT & HOW IT WORKS

A sure-fire way to exponentially decrease your time to Arabic fluency is to role play with key words and phrases that naturally occur in actual scenarios you experience on a daily basis.

This book has 50 examples of conversations, written in both Arabic and English so you never feel lost in translation, and will ensure you boost your conversational skills quickly.

You will find each chapter different from the last as two or more characters interact in real life scenarios. You will soon learn how to ask for directions, send a package at the post office, call for help, introduce yourself and even order at a restaurant.

Sometimes a direct translation does not make sense in to and from each language. Therefore, we recommend that you read each story in both languages to ensure understanding what is taking place.

Tips for Success

No doubt you can pick up this book at anytime to reference a situation that you may be in. However, in order to get the most out of this book, there is an effective approach to yield the best results.

1. **Role-play:** Learning takes place when activities are engaging and memorable. Role-play is any speaking activity when you either put yourself into someone else's shoes, or when put yourself into an imaginary situation and act it out.
2. **Look up vocab:** At some points there may be a word or phrase that you don't understand and that's completely fine. As we mentioned before, some of the translations are not word-for-word in order for the conversations to remain realistic in each language. Therefore, we recommend that you look up anything that is not fully clear to you.
3. **Create your own conversations:** After going through all of the stories we invite you to create your own by modifying what you already read. Perhaps you order additional items while at a restaurant or maybe you have an entirely different conversation over the phone. Let your imagination run wild.
4. **Seek out more dialogues:** Don't let your learning stop here. We encourage you to practice in as many ways as possible. Referencing your newly learned phrases and vocabulary, you can test your comprehension with Arabic movies and television shows. Practice, practice, practice will give you the boost to fluency.

Focus on building your foundation of words and phrases commonly used in the real world and we promise your results will be staggering! Now, go out into the world, speak with confidence and in no time native speakers will be amazed by your Arabic speaking skills.

Good luck!

SURVIVAL PHRASES

Greetings

1. *Hi!*
   Salam! – سلام

2. *Good morning!*
   Sabah el kheer - صباح الخير

3. *Good evening!*
   Masaa el kheer - مساء الخير

4. *How are you?*
   Kaifa haloka / haloki (female) - كيف حالك؟

5. *I'm fine, thanks!*
   Ana bekhair, shokran! - أنا بخير شكرا

6. *And you?*
   Wa ant? / Wa anti? (female) - و أنت؟

7. *Good / So-So.*
   Jayed / 'aadee - جيد / عادي

8. *Thank you (very much)!*
   Shokran (jazeelan) - شكرا (جزيلا)

9. *You're welcome! (for "thank you")*
   Al'afw – العفو

10. *I missed you so much!*
    Eshtaqto elaika / elaiki (female) katheeran - إشتقت إليك كثيرا

11. *What's new?*
    Maljadeed? - مالجديد؟

12. *Nothing much*
Lashai jadeed - لا شيء جديد

13. *Good night!*
Tosbeho / tosbeheena (female) 'ala khair/ - تصبح/ تصبحين على خير

14. *See you later!*
Araka / Araki (female) fi ma ba'd - أراك في مابعد

15. *Good bye!*
Ma'a salama - مع السلامة

16. *Hey! Friend!*
Ahlan sadiqi / sadiqati! (female) - أهلا صديقي /صديقتي!

17. *Welcome! (to greet someone)*
Marhaban – مرحبا

18. *You're very kind!*
Anta lateef / Anti lateefa - أنت لطيف! أنتِ لطيفة!

Introductions

1. *Do you speak (English / Arabic)?*
   Hal tatakallamu alloghah alenjleziah / alarabiah? - ***هل تتكلم اللغة الإنجليزية/العربية؟***

2. *Just a little.*
   Qaleelan! - ***قليلا!***

3. *What's your name?*
   Ma esmouk? Ma esmouki? - ***ما إسمك؟***

4. *My name is ...*
   Esmee... - ***إسمي....***

5. *Nice to meet you!*
   Motasharefon / motasharefatun (female) bema'refatek - ***متشرف / متشرفة بمعرفتك***

6. *Where are you from?*
   Men ayna anta / anti (female)? - ***من أين أنت؟***

7. *I'm American*
   Ana amreeki / amrekiah (female) - ***أنا أمريكي/أمريكية***

8. *I'm from (the U.S / Morocco)*
   Ana men (amreeka/ almaghrib) - ***أنا من (أمريكا/ المغرب)***

9. *Where do you live?*
   Ayna taskun? / Ayna taskuneen? (female) - ***أين تسكن؟ أين تسكنين؟***

10. *I live in (the U.S / France)*
    A'eesho fel welayat almotaheda / faransa - ***أعيش في الولايات المتحدة/ فرنسا***

11. *Do you like it here?*
Hal istamta'ta bewaqtika / bewaqtiki (female) huna? - هل استمتعت بوقتك هنا؟

12. *What do you do for a living?*
Ma mehnatuk? Mehnatuki (female) - ما مهنتك؟

13. *I like Arabic*
Ohibbu allughah al arabia - أحب اللغة العربية

14. *Oh! That's good!*
Hada shay'un Jameel - هذا شيء جميل

15. *I have been learning Arabic for 1 month*
adrusu allughah al arabia mundu shahr - أدرس اللغة العربية منذ شهر

16. *How old are you?*
Kam howa umruk? umroki (female) - كم هو عمرك؟

17. *I have to go!*
Yajebu an athhaba al aan! - يجب أن اذهب الآن

18. *I will be right back!*
Sa arje'o halan - سأرجع حالا

Asking for Directions

1. *I'm lost*
   Ada'tu tareeqi! - أضعت طريقي! أضعت طريقي!

2. *Can I help you?*
   Hal beemkani mosa'adatuk? - هل بإمكاني مساعدتك؟

3. *Can you help me?*
   Hal beemkanek mosa'adati? - هل بإمكانك مساعدتي؟

4. *One moment please!*
   Lahda men fadlek / fadleki (female) - لحظة من فضلك

5. *Where is the (bathroom / pharmacy)?*
   Ayna ajedu (al merhaad / assaidaliah)? - أين أجد (المرحاض/ الصيدلية)؟

6. *Go straight! Then turn left / right!*
   imshy ala tool, thumma 'arrij yaminan / shimalan - أمشِ على طول ثم عرّج يمينا/ شمالا!

7. *How much is this?*
   Kam howa thamanoh? - كم هو ثمنه؟

8. *Excuse me ...! (to ask for something)*
   Men fathlek / fathleki (female) (th as in that) - من فضلك

9. *Come with me!*
   Ta'ala / ta'alay (female) ma'ee! - تعال معي!

10. *Excuse me! (to pass by)*
    Alma'derah - المعذرة

Solving Misunderstandings

1. *I'm sorry! (if you don't hear something)*
   'Afwan! - !عفواً

2. *No problem!*
   La moshkelah - لامشكلة

3. *Sorry (for a mistake)*
   Aasef! - !أسف

4. *Can you say it again?*
   A'ed men fadlek! / A'eedi men fadleki (fem) - أعد من فضلك

5. *Can you speak slowly?*
   Takalam bebot' men fadlek/ fadleki (fem) - تكلم ببطء من فضلك

6. *I don't understand!*
   La afham! - !لا أفهم

7. *I don't know!*
   La a'ref! - !لآ أعرف

8. *I have no idea.*
   La adri! - لاأدري

9. *Write it down please!*
   Oktobha men fadlek / Oktobiha men fadleki (female) - أكتبها من فضلك! / أكتبيها من فضلك

10. *What's that called in Arabic?*
    Ma esmoho bel arabiah? - ما أسمه بالعربية؟

11. *How Do You Say "Please" in Arabic?*
Kaifa taqoulu kalimat "please" bel arabia? - **كيف تقول كلمة "بليز" بالعربية؟**

12. *I need to practice my Arabic*
Ahtaaju an atadarraba 'ala al arabia! - **احتاج ان اتدرب على العربية**

13. *What is this?*
Ma hatha - **ما هذا؟**

14. *Don't worry!*
La taqlaq! La taqlaqi (fem) - **لاتقلق / لا تقلقي!**

1. تحية رسمية – Formal Introduction
(tḥyẗ rsmyẗ)

جون : صباح الخير أستاذ جاستين، كيف حالك؟
ğwn: ṣbāḥ ālẖyr ʾstāḏ ğāstyn ،kyf ḥālk؟

بروفيسور جاستين: صباح الخير جون، أنا بخير وأنت؟
brwfyswr ğāstyn: ṣbāḥ ālẖyr ğwnʾ ،nā bẖyr wʾnt؟

جون: أنا بخير , شكرًا. هذه صديقتي كلاريسا. إنّها تفكر بالالتحاق بهذه الجامعة.هل تستطيع أن تحدثنا عن الإجراءات من فضلك؟
ğwn: ʾnā bẖyr، škrā̃. hḏh ṣdyqty klārysā. ʾnhā tfkr bālālthāq bhḏh ālğāmʿẗ.hl tsttyʿ ʾn tḥdṯnā ʿn ālʾğrāʾāt mn fḍlk؟

بروفيسور جاستين: أهلًا كلاريسا! تشرَّفت بلقائكِ وأنا سعيد جدًّا للتحدث معكِ. يمكنكِ أن تتصلي بي في مكتبي الأسبوع المقبل.
brwfyswr ğāstyn: ʾhlā̃ klārysā! tšrf̃t blqāئk.wʾnā sʿyd ğdā̃ lltḥdṯ mʿk. ymknk.ʾn ttṣly by fy mktby ālʾsbwʿ ālmqbl.

كلاريسا: سُعِدت بلقائك أستاذ. شكرًا لك على مساعدتنا.
klārysā: sʿdt blqāئk ʾstāḏ. škrā̃ lk ʿlى msāʿdtnā.

بروفيسور جاستين: بالتاكيد. آمل أن أكون قادرًا على الإجابة على أسئلتك!
brwfyswr ğāstyn: bāltākyd. ʾ̄ml ʾn ʾkwn qādrā̃ ʿlى ālʾğābẗ ʿlʾ ىsئltk!

Formal Greeting

John: Good morning, Professor Justin, how are you doing?

Professor Justin: Good morning, John. I am doing well. And you?

John: I'm well, thank you. This is my friend Clarissa. She is thinking about applying to this university. She has a few questions. Would you mind telling us about the process, please?

Professor Justin: Hello, Clarissa! It's a pleasure to meet you. I'm more than happy to speak with you. Please stop by my office next week.

Clarissa: It's a pleasure to meet you, professor. Thank you so much for helping us.

Professor Justin: Of course. Hopefully, I will be able to answer your questions!

2. تحية غير رسمية - Informal Greeting
(tḥyẗ ġyr rsmyẗ)

جيف: من هي المرأة الطويلة التي بجانب باربرا؟
ğyf: mn hy ālmrʾẗ ālṭwylẗ ālty bğānb bārbrā؟

تشارلز: إنَّها صديقتها ماري. ألم تقابلها في حفلة ستيف؟
tšārlz: ʾnhā ṣdyqthā māry. ʾlm tqāblhā fy ḥflẗ styf؟

جيف: لا, لم أحضر حفلة ستيف.
ğyf: lā, lm ʾḥḍr ḥflẗ styf.

تشارلز: أوه! إذًا دعني أقدمك لها الآن. ماري، هذا صديقي جيف.
tšārlz: ʾwh! ʾḏā dʿny ʾqdmk lhā ālʾn. māry ،hḏā ṣdyqy ğyf.

ماري: مرحبًا، جيف. تشرَّفت بمقابلتك.
māry: mrḥbā ،ğyf. tšrft bmqābltk.

جيف: وأنا أيضًا. هل ترغبين بأن تحتسي معي شرابًا؟
ğyf: wʾnā ʾyḍā. hl trġbyn bʾn tḥtsy mʿy šrābā؟

ماري: بالتأكيد، لنذهب ونحصل على واحد.
māry: bāltʾkyd ،lnḏhb wnḥṣl ʿlى wāḥd.

Informal Greeting

Jeff: Who's the tall woman next to Barbara?

Charles: That's her friend Mary. Didn't you meet her at Steve's party?

Jeff: No, I wasn't at Steve's party.

Charles: Oh! Then let me introduce you to her now. Mary, this is my friend Jeff.

Mary: Hi, Jeff. Nice to meet you.

Jeff: You, too. Would you like a drink?

Mary: Sure, let's go get one.

3. مكالمة هاتفية – A TELEPHONE CALL
(mkālmᶦ hātfyᶦ)

جون: مرحبًا أليس، أنا جون. كيف حالك؟
ǧwn: mrḥbā̄ ˡlysˡ ‹nā ǧwn. kyf ḥālk؟

أليس: أوه، مرحبًا، جون! لقد كنت أفكر بك.
ˡlys: ˡwh ‹mrḥbā̄ ‹ǧwn! lqd knt ˡfkr bk.

جون: رائع. كنتُ أتساءل إذا كنتِ ترغبين أن نذهب لمشاهدة فيلم الليلة.
ǧwn: rāئʿ. knt ˡtsāʾl ˡḏā knt trġbyn ˡn nḏhb lmšāhdᶦ fylm āllylᶦ.

أليس: بالتأكيد، أود ذلك! ماهو الفيلم الذي تريد مشاهدته؟
ˡlys: bāltˡkydˡ ‹wd ḏlk! māhw ālfylm ālḏy tryd mšāhdth؟

جون: كنت أفكر في الفيلم الكوميدي الجديد Turn Off the Lights. ما رأيك؟
ǧwn: knt ˡfkr fy ālfylm ālkwmydy ālǧdydTurn Off the Lights . mā rˡyk؟

أليس: عظيم!
ˡlys: ʿẓym!

جون: حسنًا، سآخذك حوالي الساعة 7:30. فالفيلم يبدأ في الساعة 8:00.
ǧwn: ḥsnā̄ ‹sˡḫḏk ḥwāly ālsāʿ7:30 ᶦ. fālfylm ybdˡ fy ālsāʿ8:00 ᶦ.

أليس: أراك لاحقًا إذًا. وداعًا!
ˡlys: ˡrāk lāḥqā̄ ˡḏā̄. wdāʿā̄!

A TELEPHONE CALL

John: Hi, Alice, it's John. How are you?

Alice: Oh, hi, John! I was just thinking about you.

John: That's nice. I was wondering if you'd like to go to a movie tonight.

Alice: Sure, I'd love to! Which movie do you want to see?

John: I was thinking about that new comedy *Turn Off the Lights.* What do you think?

Alice: Sounds great!

John: Ok, I'll pick you up around 7:30. The movie starts at 8:00.

Alice: See you then. Bye!

4. كم الساعة الان؟ – What Time Is It?

(km ālsāʿ̈ ālān؟)

ناتاشا: كم الساعة الآن؟ سوف نكون متأخرين!

nātāšā: km ālsāʿ̈ ālʾn؟ swf nkwn mtʾẖryn!

توني: إنها السابعة والربع. نحن في الوقت. لا داعي للخوف.

twny: ʾnhā ālsābʿ̈ wālrbʿ. nḥn fy ālwqt. lā dāʿy llẖwf.

ناتاشا: ولكن أعتقد أنه كان علينا أن نكون في المطعم على الساعة 7:30 للحفلة المفاجئة. لن نستطيع أن نكون هناك في الوقت مع كل هذا الزحام في المساء.

nātāšā: wlkn ʾʿtqd ʾnh kān ʿlynā ʾn nkwn fy ālmṭʿm ʿlى ālsāʿ7:30 ̈ llḥfl̈ ālmfāǧئ̈. ln nsttṭyʿ ʾn nkwn hnāk fy ālwqt mʿ kl hḏā ālzḥām fy ālmsāʾ.

توني: أنا متأكد من أننا سنفعلها. انتهت ساعة الذروة تقريبًا. على أي حال، الحفل يبدأ في الساعة 8:00. لكنني بحاجة لمساعدة في إرشادات الطريق. هل يمكنكِ أن تتصلي بالمطعم وتطلبي منه مكانًا لحجز سيارتنا؟

twny: ʾnā mtʾkd mn ʾnnā snfʿlhā. āntht sāʿ̈ ālḏrẅ tqrybā̋. ʿlʾ ى y ḥāl ،ālḥfl ybdʾ fy ālsāʿ8:00 ̈. lknny bḥāǧ̈ lmsāʿd̈ fy ʾršādāt ālṭryq. hl ymknkِ ʾn ttṣly bālmṭʿm wtṭlby mnh mkānā̋ lḥǧz syārtnā؟

ناتاشا: بالطبع.

nātāšā: bālṭbʿ.

What Time Is It?

Natasha: What time is it? We're going to be late!

Tony: It's a quarter after seven. We're on time. Don't panic.

Natasha: But I thought we had to be at the restaurant by 7:30 for the surprise party. We'll never make it there with all this evening traffic.

Tony: I'm sure we will. Rush hour is almost over. Anyway, the party starts at 8:00.

But I do need help with directions. Can you call the restaurant and ask them where we park our car?

Natasha: Of course.

5. هل يمكنك قول ذلك مجددًا؟ – CAN YOU SAY THAT AGAIN?

(**hl ymknk qwl ḏlk mǧddā̈؟**)

لوك: مرحبًا؟ مرحبًا ستيفاني، كيف تسير الأمور في المكتب؟

lwk: mrḥbā̈؟ mrḥbā̈ styfāny ،kyf tsyr āl꞉mwr fy ālmktb؟

ستيفاني: مرحبًا لوك! كيف حالك؟ هل يمكنك التوقف عند المتجر وشراء بعض الورق الإضافي للطابعة؟

styfāny: mrḥbā̈ lwk! kyf ḥālk؟ hl ymknk āltwqf ʿnd ālmtǧr wšrāʾ bʿḍ ālwrq āl꞉ḍāfy llṭābʿ؟ة

لوك: ماذا قلتِ؟ هل يمكنكِ أن تعيدي ما قلتِ من فضلك؟ هل قلتِ لالتقاط الحبر للطابعة؟ عفوًا فان الهاتف يقطع.

lwk: māḏā qlt؟ hl ymknk꞉n tʿydy mā qlt mn fḍlk؟ hl qlt lāltqāṭ ālḥbr llṭābʿ؟ة ʿfwā̈ fān ālhātf yqṭʿ.

ستيفاني: هل تسمعني الآن؟ لا، أنا بحاجة إلى المزيد من أوراق الكمبيوتر. اسمع، سأكتب لك ما أحتاجه بالضبط. شكرًا، لوك. سوف أتحدث إليك لاحقًا.

styfāny: hl tsmʿny āl꞉n؟ lā꞉ ،nā bḥāǧ꞉ ىاة ālmzyd mn ꞉wrāq ālkmbywtr. āsmʿ ،s꞉ktb lk mā ꞉ḥtāǧh bālḍbṭ. škrā̈ ،lwk. swf ꞉tḥdṯ ꞉lyk lāḥqā̈.

لوك: شكرًا، ستيفاني. عذرًا فان استقبال هاتفي سيء جدًّا هنا.

lwk: škrā̈ ،styfāny. ʿḏrā̈ fān āstqbāl hātfy syʾ ǧdā̈ hnā.

Can You Say That Again?

Luke: Hello? Hi, Stephanie, how are things at the office?

Stephanie: Hi, Luke! How are you? Can you please stop the store and pick up extra paper for the printer?

Luke: What did you say? Can you repeat that, please? Did you say to pick up ink for the printer? Sorry, the phone is cutting out.

Stephanie: Can you hear me now? No, I need more computer paper. Listen, I'll text you exactly what I need. Thanks, Luke.

Talk to you later.

Luke: Thanks, Stephanie. Sorry, my phone has really bad

reception here.

6. مصادفات – Coincidences
(mṣādfāt)

ميج: مرحبًا جوليا! لم أركِ منذ وقت طويل!
myğ: mrḥbā̈ ğwlyā! lm ʾrk mnḏ wqt ṭwyl!

جوليا: ميج! مرحبًا! يالها من صدفة! لم أشاهدكِ منذ أمد طويل! ماذا تفعلين هنا؟
ğwlyā: myğ! mrḥbā̈! yālhā mn ṣdfẗ! lm ʾšāhdk mnḏ ʾmd ṭwyl! māḏā tfʿlyn hnā؟

ميج: لقد حصلت للتو على وظيفة جديدة في المدينة، لذلك فأنا أتسوق لشراء بعض الملابس. مهلًا، ما رأيكِ في هذا القميص؟
myğ: lqd ḥṣlt lltw ʿlى wẓyfẗ ğdydẗ fy ālmdyn ،ẗlḏlk fʾnā ʾtswq lšrāʾ bʿḍ ālmlābs. mhlā̈ ،mā rʾyk fy hḏā ālqmyṣ؟

جوليا: هممم ... جيد، أنتِ تعرفين كم أعشق اللون الأزرق. انظري؟ لدي نفس القميص !
ğwlyā: hmmm ... ğydʾ ،nt tʿrfyn km ʾʿšq āllwn ālʾzrq. ānẓry؟ ldy nfs ālqmyṣ!

ميج: إنه لطالما كان لديكِ ذوق جيد! يا له من عالم صغير.
myğ: ʾnh lṭālmā kān ldyk ḏwq ğyd! yā lh mn ʿālm ṣġyr.

COINCIDENCES

Meg: Well, hello there, Julia! Long time no see!

Julia: Meg! Hi! What a coincidence! I haven't seen you in forever! What are you doing here?

Meg: I just got a new job in the city, so I'm shopping for some clothes. Hey, what do you think of this shirt?

Julia: Hmmm... Well, you know how much I love blue. See? I've got the same shirt!

Meg: You always did have good taste! What a small world.

7. الطقس – The Weather
(ālṭqs)

سالي: الجو بارد في الخارج! ماذا حدث لنشرة الطقس؟ كنت أعتقد أنه من المفترض أن تمر موجة البرد هذه.
sāly: ālǧw bārd fy ālẖārǧ! mādā ḥdṯ lnšrẗ ālṭqs؟ knt ̉ʿtqd ̉nh mn ālmftrḍ ̉n tmr mwǧẗ ālbrd hḏh.

غابرييلا: صحيح, أنا مثلك .هذا ما قرأته على الإنترنت في هذا الصباح.
ġābryylā: ṣḥyḥ، ̉nā mṯlk. hḏā mā qr̉th ʿlى āl̹ntrnt fy hḏā ālṣbāḥ.

سالي :أعتقد أن عاصفة الريح أدت إلى انخفاض درجة الحرارة.
sāly: ̉ʿtqd ̉n ʿāṣfẗ ālryḥ ̉dt ̹lى ānẖfāḍ drǧẗ ālḥrārẗ.

غابرييلا: هل يمكننا الدخول؟ أشعر أن أصابع قدمي أصابها الشلل.
ġābryylā: hl ymknnā āldẖwl؟ ̉šʿr ̉n ̉ṣābʿ qdmy ̉ṣābhā ālšll.

The Weather

Sally: It's freezing outside! What happened to the weather report? I thought this cold front was supposed to pass.

Gabriela: Yeah, I thought so too. That's what I read online this morning.

Sally: I guess the wind chill is really driving down the temperature.

Gabriela: Can we go inside? I feel like my toes are starting to go numb.

8. طلب الطعام - Ordering Food
(ṭlb ālṭʿām)

النادل: مرحبًا بك، سأكون في خدمتك اليوم. يمكنك أن تبدأ بشيء تشربه؟
ālnādl: mrḥbā̆ bk ،sأkwn fy ẖdmtk ālywm. ymknk أn tbdأ bšyʾ tšrbh؟

شون: نعم. شاي مثلج من فضلك.
šwn: nʿm. šāy mṯlǧ mn fḍlk.

آنا: أمّا أنا فسآخذ عصير ليمون من فضلك.
آnā: أmā̆ أnā fsآẖḏ ʿṣyr lymwn mn fḍlk.

النادل: جيد. هل ستطلبان الآن أم أنّكما تحتاجان إلى بضع دقائق؟
ālnādl: ǧyd. hl stṭlbān ālآn أm أnkmā tḥtāǧān إlى bḍʿ dqāئq؟

شون: أعتقد أننا جاهزان. سآخذ حساء الطماطم في البداية، ولحم البقر المشوي مع البطاطس المهروسة والبازلاء.
šwn: أʿtqd أnnā ǧāhzān. sآẖḏ ḥsāʾ ālṭmāṭm fy ālbdāyة، wlḥm ālbqr ālmšwy mʿ ālbṭāṭs ālmhrwsة wālbāzlāʾ.

النادل: كيف تريد لحم البقر قليلة الاستواء، أم متوسطة، أم ناضجة جدا؟
ālnādl: kyf tryd lḥm ālbqr qlylة ālāstwāʾأ ،m mtwsṭأ ،ةm nāḍǧة ǧdā؟

شون: ناضجة جدًّا، من فضلك.
šwn: nāḍǧة ǧdā̆ ،mn fḍlk.

آنا: أمّا أنا فسآخذ فقط السمك مع البطاطا والسلطة.
آnā: أmā̆ أnā fsآẖḏ fqṭ ālsmk mʿ ālbṭāṭā wālslṭة.

ORDERING FOOD

Waiter: Hello, I'll be your waiter today. Can I start you off with something to drink?

Sean: Yes. I would like iced tea, please.

Anna: And I'll have lemonade., please.

Waiter: Ok. Are you ready to order, or do you need a few minutes?

Sean: I think we're ready. I'll have the tomato soup to start, and the roast beef with mashed potatoes and peas.

Waiter: How do you want the beef — rare, medium, or well done?

Sean: Well done, please.

Anna: And I'll just have the fish, with potatoes and a salad.

9. موعد مع الطبيب – VISITING THE DOCTOR

(mwʿd mʿ ālṭbyb)

الطبيب: ما المشكلة؟

kāṯy: ḥsnā̋... ldy sʿāl šdyd wĪlām fy ālḥlq bāl!ḍāf! ةاﻯ ālṣdāʿ.

كاثي: حسنًا... لدي سعال شديد وآلام في الحلق بالإضافة إلى الصداع.

ālṭbyb: mnḏ mtﻯ bdt ʿlykِ hḏh ālʾʿrāḍ؟

الطبيب: منذ متى بدت عليكِ هذه الأعراض؟

kāṯy: mnḏ ḥwāly ṯlāṯʾ ةyām. wʾnā ʾyḍā̋ mrhqة.

كاثي: منذ حوالي ثلاثة أيام. وأنا أيضًا مرهقة.

kāṯy: mnḏ ḥwāly ṯlāṯʾ ةyām. wʾnā ʾyḍā̋ mrhqة.

الطبيب: هممم... يبدو أنكِ مصابة بالأنفلونزا. خذي الأسبرين كل أربع ساعات واحصلي على الكثير من الراحة. احرصي على شرب الكثير من السوائل. أعيدي الاتصال بي إذا كنتِ لا تزالين مريضة الأسبوع القادم.

ālṭbyb: hmmm... ybdw ʾnkِ mṣābة bālʾnflwnzā. ẖḏy ālʾsbryn kl ʾrbʿ sāʿāt wāḥṣly ʿlﻯ ālkṯyr mn ālrāḥة. āḥrṣy ʿlﻯ šrb ālkṯyr mn ālswāﺋl. ʾʿydy ālātṣāl by !ḏā kntِ lā tzālyn mryḍة ālʾsbwʿ ālqādm.

كاثي: حسنًا، شكرًا لك.

kāṯy: ḥsnā̋ ،škrā̋ lk.

VISITING THE DOCTOR

Doctor: What seems to be the problem?

Cathy: Well… I have a bad cough and a sore throat. I also have a headache.

Doctor: How long have you had these symptoms?

Cathy: About three days now. And I'm really tired, too.

Doctor: Hmm. It sounds like you've got the flu. Take aspirin every four hours and get plenty of rest. Make sure you drink lots of fluids. Call me if you're still sick next week.

Cathy: Ok, thank you.

10. السؤال عن الاتجاهات – ASKING FOR DIRECTIONS
(ālsؤāl ʿn ālātǧāhāt)

مارك: عفوًا, هل يمكن أن تخبريني أين هي المكتبة؟
mārk: ʿfwًā، hl ymkn أn tẖbryny أyn hy ālmktbة؟

أوليفيا: نعم، إنها من هنا. يمكنك المشي ثلاثة احياء إلى شارع واشنطن، ثم الانعطاف يمينًا. سوف تجدها في الزاوية، قبالة البنك.
أwlyfyā: nʿm، إnhā mn hnā. ymknk ālmšy ṯlāṯة āḥyāʾ إlى šārʿ wāšnṭn، ṯm ālānʿṭāf ymynًā. swf tǧdhā fy ālzāwyة، qbālة ālbnk.

مارك: شكرًا! أنا في المدينة منذ بضعة أيام، لذلك لا أعرف الطريق حتى الآن.
mārk: škrًā! أnā fy ālmdynة mnḏ bḍʿة أyām، lḏlk lā أʿrf ālṭryq ḥtى ālآn.

أوليفيا: أوه، أنا أعرف كيف تشعر. انتقلنا العام الماضي، وما زلت لا أعرف مكان كل شيء!
أwlyfyā: أwh، أnā أʿrf kyf tšʿr. āntqlnā ālʿām ālmāḍy، wmā zlt lā أʿrf mkān kl šyʾ!

Asking For Directions

Marc: Excuse me. Could you tell me where the library is?

Olivia: Yes, it's that way. You go three blocks to Washington Street, then turn right. It's on the corner, across from the bank.

Marc: Thanks! I've only been in town a few days, so I really don't know my way around yet.

Olivia: Oh, I know how you feel. We moved here a year ago, and I still don't know where everything is!

11. طلب المساعدة – CALLING FOR HELP
(ṭlb ālmsāʿdᵒ)

بيتر: مرحبًا! تلك السيارة تجاوزت الضوء الأحمر واصطدمت بتلك الشاحنة!
bytr: mrḥbā̃! tlk ālsyārᵒ tǧāwzt ālḍwʾ ālꜣḥmr wāṣṭdmt btlk ālšāḥnᵒ!

غيل: هل أصيب أي أحد؟
ġyl: hl ꜣṣyb ꜣy ꜣḥd؟

بيتر: لا أعرف ... دعنا نتصل بال 911... مرحبًا, أود الإبلاغ عن حادث سيارة بالقرب من مكتب البريد في شارع هيوستن. يبدو أن هناك رجل مصاب. نعم، لقد حدث للتو. شكرًا، وداعًا.
bytr: lā ꜣʿrf .. dʿnā ntṣl bāl 911... mrḥbā̃، ꜣwd ālꜣblāġ ʿn ḥādṯ syārᵒ bālqrb mn mktb ālbryd fy šārʿ hywstn. ybdw ꜣn hnāk rǧl mṣāb. nʿm ،lqd ḥdṯ lltw. škrā̃ ،wdāʿā̃.

غيل: ماذا قالوا لك؟
ġyl: māḏā qālwā lk؟

بيتر: سيرسلون سيارة إسعاف وسيارة شرطة على الفور.
bytr: syrslwn syārꜣ ᵒsʿāf wsyārᵒ šrṭᵒ ʿlى ālfwr.

غيل: جيد، إنهم هنا. آمل أن يكون الرجل على ما يرام.
ġyl: ǧydꜣ ،nhm hnā. ꜣ̄ml ꜣn ykwn ālrǧl ʿlى mā yrām.

بيتر: أعرف. يجب أن تتحلى بالحذر الشديد عند القيادة.
bytr: ꜣʿrf. yǧb ꜣn ttḥlى bālḥḏr ālšdyd ʿnd ālqyādᵒ.

Calling For Help

Peter: Hey! That car just ran a red light and hit that truck!

Gail: Is anyone hurt?

Peter: I don't know... let's call 911. ...Hello? I'd like to report a car accident near the post office on Houston Street. It looks like a man is hurt. Yes, it just happened. Ok, thanks. Bye.

Gail: What did they say?

Peter: They're going to send an ambulance and a police car right away.

Gail: Good, they're here. I hope the man is alright.

Peter: I know. You have to be so careful when you're driving.

12. التسوق – SHOPPING

(āltswq)

لويز: مرحبًا جوليا ... انظري إلى تلك المقبلات! ما رأيكِ أن نخبز كوكيز اليوم؟

lwyz: mrḥbā̃ ğwlyā ... ānẓry !lى tlk ālmqblāt! mā rʾyk.ʾn nẖbz kwkyz ālywm؟

جوليا: هممم ... حسنًا، إنها فكرة رائعة! بينما نحن هنا, هيّا نشتري المكونات.

ğwlyā: hmmm ... ḥsnā̃! ،nhā fkrة rāئعة! bynmā nḥn hnā، hyā̃ nštry ālmkwnāt.

جوليا: حسنًا، ماذا نحتاج؟

ğwlyā: ḥsnā̃ ،māḏā nḥtāğ؟

لويز: نحتاج إلى الطحين والسكر والزبدة. أوه، ونحتاج أيضًا إلى البيض ورقائق الشيكولاتة.

lwyz: nḥtāğ !lى ālṭḥyn wālskr wālzbdا .ةwh ،wnḥtāğ ʾyḍā̃ !lى ālbyḍ wrqāئq ālšykwlātة.

جوليا: لماذا لا تحصلين على الألبان؟ ستجدينها في القسم المبرد في الجزء الخلفي من المتجر. سأحصل على المكونات الجافة. أعتقد أنهم في الممر رقم 10.

ğwlyā: lmāḏā lā tḥṣlyn ʿlى ālʾlbān؟ stğdynhā fy ālqsm ālmbrd fy ālğzʾ ālẖlfy mn ālmtğr. sʾḥṣl ʿlى ālmkwnāt ālğāfا .ةʿtqd ʾnhm fy ālmmr rqm 10.

لويز: حسنًا! لنلتقي عند ممر الخروج.

lwyz: ḥsnā̃! lnltqy ʿnd mmr ālẖrwğ.

جوليا: حسنًا. أراكِ هناك.

ğwlyā: ḥsnā̃. ʾrāk.hnāk.

SHOPPING

Louise: Hey, Julia... Look at those desserts! How about baking some cookies today?

Julia: Hmm... Yeah, that's a great idea! While we're here, let's pick up the ingredients.

Julia: Ok, what do we need?

Louise: The recipe calls for flour, sugar and butter. Oh, and we also need eggs and chocolate chips.

Julia: Why don't you get the dairy ingredients? You'll find those in the refrigerated section in the back of the store. I'll get the dry ingredients. I believe they're in aisle 10.

Louise: Great! Let's meet at the checkout.

Julia: Ok. See you there.

13. إدارة المهمات – Running Errands
(ḷdārᵒ ālmhmāt)

موظف استقبال الفندق: مرحبًا بكم. كيف يمكنني مساعدتك؟

mwẓf āstqbāl ālfndq: mrḥbā̈ bkm. kyf ymknny msāʿdtk؟

كلير: حسنًا، أنا في زيارة للمدينة لبضعة أيام، وأحتاج إلى إنجاز بعض المهام أثناء وجودي هنا.

klyr: ḥsnā̈ỉ ،nā fy zyārᵒ llmdynᵒ lbḍʿỉ ᵒyām ،wỉḥtāğ ḷlḷ ىnğāz bʿḍ ālmhām ỉṯnāʾ wğwdy hnā.

موظف استقبال الفندق: طبعًا. ماذا تحتاجين؟

mwẓf āstqbāl ālfndq: ṭbʿā̈. mādā tḥtāğyn؟

كلير: أريد أن أحصل على قصة شعر. كما أني بحاجة إلى تطويق سروالي.

klyr: ỉryd ỉn ỉḥṣl ʿlى qṣᵒ šʿr. kmā ỉny bḥāğḷ ᵒlى tṭwyq srwāly.

موظف استقبال الفندق: حسنًا. إليكِ خريطة للمدينة. يوجد صالون لتصفيف الشعر هنا، وهو على بعد حي واحد فقط من هنا. وأيضًا يوجد خياط هنا. هل يوجد هناك شيء آخر؟

mwẓf āstqbāl ālfndq: ḥsnā̈. ḷlyk ẖryṭᵒ llmdynᵒ. ywğd ṣālwn ltṣfyf ālšʿr hnā ،whw ʿlى bʿd ḥy wāḥd fqṭ mn hnā. wỉyḍā̈ ywğd ẖyāṭ hnā. hl ywğd hnāk šyʾ ỉẖr؟

كلير: نعم. سأحتاج إلى صيانة سيارتي قبل مغادرتي!

klyr: nʿm. sỉḥtāğ ḷlى ṣyānᵒ syārty qbl mġādrty!

موظف استقبال الفندق: لا مشكلة. يوجد ميكانيكي جيد على بعد بضعة أحياء.

mwẓf āstqbāl ālfndq: lā mšklᵒ. ywğd mykānyky ğyd ʿlى bʿd bḍʿ ᵒ ỉḥyāʾ.

Running Errands

Hotel receptionist: Hello there. How can I help you?

Claire: Well, I'm in town visiting for a few days, and I need to get some things done while I'm here.

Hotel receptionist: Sure. What do you need?

Claire: I need to get my hair cut. I also need to have my new pants hemmed.

Hotel receptionist: Ok. Here's a map of the city. There's a good hair salon here, which is just a block away. And there's a tailor right here. Is there anything else?

Claire: Yes. I'll need to get my car serviced before my long drive back home!

Hotel receptionist: No problem. There's a good mechanic a few blocks away.

14. في مكتب البريد – AT THE POST OFFICE
(fy mktb ālbryd)

موظف البريد: كيف يمكنني مساعدتك اليوم؟
mwẓf ālbryd: kyf ymknny msāʿdtk ālywm؟

كارول: أريد إرسال هذه الحزمة إلى نيويورك من فضلك.
kārwl: ỉryd ỉrsāl hḏh ālḥzmۃ ỉlى nywywrk mn fḍlk.

موظف البريد: جيد، لنرى كم تزن ... إنها حوالي خمسة أرطال. إذا قمتِ بإرسالها بسرعة، فستصل إلى هناك غدًا. أو يمكنكِ إرسالها بالأولوية وستصل إلى هناك بحلول يوم السبت.
mwẓf ālbryd: ǧyd، lnrى km tzn ... ỉnhā ḥwāly ḫmsۃ ảrṭāl. ỉḏā qmtِ bỉrsālhā bsrʿۃ، fstṣl ỉlى hnāk ġdًā. ảw ymknkِ ỉrsālhā bālảwlwyۃ wstṣl ỉlى hnāk bḥlwl ywm ālsbt.

كارول: السبت جيد. كم تكلفة ذلك؟
kārwl: ālsbt ǧyd. km tklfۃ ḏlk؟

موظف البريد: $12.41. هل تحتاجين شيئًا آخر؟
mwẓf ālbryd: 12.41$. hl tḥtāǧyn šyỷًā ậḫr؟

كارول: نعم! كدت أن أنسى. أنا بحاجة إلى كتاب من الطوابع أيضًا.
kārwl: nʿm! kdt ản ảnsى. ảnā bḥāǧۃ ỉlى ktāb mn ālṭwābʿ ảyḍًā.

موظف البريد: حسنًا، المبلغ الإجمالي يصل إلى $18.94.
mwẓf ālbryd: ḥsnًā، ālmblġ ālỉǧmāly yṣl ỉlى 18.94$.

At The Post Office

Postal clerk: What can I help you today?

Carol: I need to mail this package to New York, please.

Postal clerk: Ok, let's see how much it weighs… it's about five pounds. If you send it express, it will get there tomorrow. Or you can send it priority and it will get there by Saturday.

Carol: Saturday is fine. How much will that be?

Postal clerk: $12.41. Do you need anything else?

Carol: Oh, yeah! I almost forgot. I need a book of stamps, too.

Postal clerk: Ok, your total comes to $18.94.

15. الامتحان – The Exam
(ālāmtḥān)

شيريل: مرحبًا! كيف كان امتحان الفيزياء؟
šyryl: mrḥbā̃! kyf kān āmtḥān ālfyzyā'؟

فرانك: ليس سيئًا، شكرًا. أنا فقط سعيد أنه انتهى! ماذا عنكِ... كيف كان تقديمك للعرض؟
frānk: lys syئā̃، škrā̃. ˡnā fqṭ sʿyd ˡnh ānthى! mādā ʿnk... kyf kān tqdymk llʿrḍ؟

شيريل: أوه، لقد سار بشكل جيد. شكرًا لمساعدتك لي في ذلك!
šyryl: ˡwh، lqd sār bškl ğyd. škrā̃ lmsāʿdtk ly fy dlk!

فرانك: لا مشكلة.. هل تريد أن ندرس غدًا لامتحان الرياضيات؟
frānk: lā mšklة.. hl tryd ˡn ndrs ġdā̃ lāmtḥān ālryāḍyāt؟

شيريل: نعم، بالتأكيد! تعال حوالي الساعة العاشرة صباحًا بعد فطور الصباح.
šyryl: nʿm ، bāltˡkyd! tʿāl ḥwāly ālsāʿة ālʿāšrة ṣbāḥā̃ bʿd fṭwr ālṣbāḥ.

فرانك: حسنًا. سوف أجلب ملاحظاتي.
frānk: ḥsnā̃. swf ˡğlb mlāḥẓāty.

The Exam

Cheryl: Hey! How did your physics exam go?

Frank: Not bad, thanks. I'm just glad it's over! How about your… how'd your presentation go?

Cheryl: Oh, it went really well. Thanks for helping me with it!

Frank: No problem. So… do you feel like studying tomorrow for our math exam?

Cheryl: Yeah, sure! Come over around 10:00 am, after breakfast.

Frank: All right. I'll bring my notes.

16. السترة المثالية – The Perfect Sweater
(ālstrꜩ ālmṯālyꜩ)

مندوب المبيعات: هل يمكنني مساعدتك؟
mndwb ālmby'āt: hl ymknny msā'dtk؟

غلوريا: نعم، أنا أبحث عن سترة- في مقاس متوسط.
ġlwryā: n'm، ˈnā ˈbḥṯ 'n str-ꜩ fy mqās mtwsṭ.

مندوب المبيعات: لنرى ... هذه واحدة بيضاء وجميلة. ما رأيكِ؟
mndwb ālmby'āt: lnrى ... hḏh wāḥdꜩ byḍā' wğmyl.ꜩ mā rˈyk؟

غلوريا: أعتقد أنّي سأحبذ أن تكون باللون الأزرق.
ġlwryā: ˈ'tqd ˈnÿ sˈḥbḏ ˈn tkwn bāllwn ālˈzrq.

مندوب المبيعات: حسنًا... هذه واحدة زرقاء، في المقاس المتوسط. هل ترغبين في تجربتها؟
mndwb ālmby'āt: ḥsnā... hḏh wāḥdꜩ zrqā'، fy ālmqās ālmtwsṭ. hl trġbyn fy tğrbthā؟

غلوريا: نعم، أنا ارغب في ذلك. إنها في مقاسي. كم سعرها؟
ġlwryā: n'm، ˈnā ārġb fy ḏlk. ˌnhā fy mqāsy. km s'rhā؟

مندوب المبيعات: إنه 41 دولار. وسيكون 50 دولار مع الضريبة.
mndwb ālmby'āt: ˌnh 41 dwlār. wsykwn 50 dwlār m' ālḍrybꜩ.

غلوريا: رائع! سوف آخذها. شكرًا!
ġlwryā: rāئ'! swf ˈḫḏhā. škrā!

THE PERFECT SWEATER

Salesperson: Can I help you?

Gloria: Yes, I'm looking for a sweater — in a size medium.

Salesperson: Let's see… here's a nice white one. What do you think?

Gloria: I think I'd rather have it in blue.

Salesperson: Ok … here's blue, in a medium. Would you

like to try it on?

Gloria: Ok … yes, I love it. It fits perfectly. How much is it?

Salesperson: It's $41. It will be $50, with tax.

Gloria: Perfect! I'll take it. Thank you!

17. سيارة أجرة أم حافلة – TAXI OR BUS
(syārة ảğrة ảm ḥāflة)

جويس: هل نأخذ سيارة أجرة أم حافلة إلى دار السينما؟
ǧwys: hl nả̇ẖḏ syārة ảğrة ảm ḥāflة ảlى dār ālsynmā?

بيل: لِنأخذ حافلة. من المستحيل أن نحصل على سيارة أجرة خلال ساعة الذروة.
byl: lnả̇ẖḏ ḥāfl.ة mn ālmstḥyl ả̇n nḥṣl 'lى syārة ảğrة ẖlāl sā'ة āldrwة.

جويس: أليس هذا موقف حافلات؟
ǧwys: ả̇lys hḏā mwqf ḥāflāt?

بيل: نعم ... أوه! هناك حافلة الآن. سيكون علينا أن نجري للحاق بها.
byl: n'm ... ả̇wh! hnāk ḥāflة āl'ā̇n. sykwn 'lynā ả̇n nğry llḥāq bhā.

جويس: أوه، لا! لقد فاتتنا للتو.
ǧwys: ả̇wh، lā! lqd fāttnā lltw.

بيل: لا مشكلة. ستكون هناك واحدة أخرى بعد 10 دقائق.
byl: lā mškl.ة stkwn hnāk wāḥdả̇ة ả̇ẖrى b'd 10 dqā'ỉq.

TAXI OR BUS

Joyce: Should we take a taxi or a bus to the movie theater?

Bill: Let's take a bus. It's impossible to get a taxi during rush hour.

Joyce: Isn't that a bus stop over there?

Bill: Yes... Oh! There's a bus now. We'll have to run to catch it.

Joyce: Oh, no! We just missed it.

Bill: No problem. There'll be another one in 10 minutes.

18. كم تبلغ من العمر؟ – HOW OLD ARE YOU?
(km tblġ mn ālʿmrʕ)

غلوريا: أنا متحمسة لحفلة عيد ميلاد العمة ماري المفاجئة بعد الظهر! وأنتِ ألستِ متحمسة؟

ġlwryā: ʾnā mtḥmsة lḥflة ʿyd mylād ālʿmة māry ālmfāğئة bʿd ālẓhr! wʾntِ ʾlstِ mtḥmsʕة

ناديا: نعم! كم تبلغ من العمر؟

nādyā: nʿm! km tblġ mn ālʿmrʕ

غلوريا: سيبلغ عمرها 55 في 5 مايو.

ġlwryā: syblġ ʿmrhā 55 fy 5 māyw.

ناديا: واو! لم أكن أعرف أن أمي أكبر - ستصبح 58 في 9 أكتوبر. على أي حال، ستفاجأ العمة ماري برؤيتنا جميعًا هنا!

nādyā: wāw! lm ʾkn ʾʿrf ʾn ʾmy ʾkbr - stṣbḥ 58 fy 9 ʾktwbr. ʿlى ʾy ḥāl، stfāğʾ ālʿmة māry brؤytnā ğmyʿًā hnā!

غلوريا: أعلم! ولكن لا يزال يجب علينا تحضير جميع الطعام قبل أن تصل إلى هنا ... حسنًا! نحن مستعدون الآن. اصمتي! إنها هنا!

ġlwryā: ʾʿlm! wlkn lā yzāl yğb ʿlynā tḥḍyr ğmyʿ ālṭʿām qbl ʾn tṣl ʾlى hnā ... ḥsnًā! nḥn mstʿdwn ālʾn. āṣmty! ʾnhā hnā!

الكل: مفاجأة!

ālkl: mfāğʾة!

How Old Are You?

Gloria: I'm really excited for Aunt Mary's surprise birthday party this afternoon! Aren't you?

Nadia: Yeah! How old is she?

Gloria: She'll be 55 on May 5.

Nadia: Wow! I didn't know that my mom was older — she's going to be 58 on October 9. Anyway, Aunt Mary's going to be so surprised to see us all here!

Gloria: I know! But we still have to get all the food set up before she gets here ... Ok! We're all ready now. Shh! She's here!

All: Surprise!

19. في المسرح – AT THE THEATER
(fy ālmsrḥ)

بوب: من فضلك، نود الحصول على تذكرتين لعرض ال 3:30.
bwb: mn fḍlk، nwd ālḥṣwl ʿlى tḏkrtyn lʿrḍ āl 3:30.

بائعة التذاكر: تفضل. استمتع بالفيلم!
bāئʿة āltḏākr: tfḍl. āstmtʿ bālfylm!

[داخل المسرح]
[dāḫl ālmsrḥ]

بوب: ألا تمانعين في الانتقال إلى المقعد الموالي، ليتسنى لنا الجلوس معًا أنا وصديقي؟
bwb: ٱlā tmānʿyn fy ālāntqāl إlى ālmqʿd ālmwāly، lytsnى lnā ālǧlws mʿاً ٱnā wṣdyqy ؟

امرأة: لا، لا مشكلة.
āmr:ٱة lā، lā mšklة.

بوب: شكرًا جزيلًا!
bwb: škrاً ǧzylاً!

At The Theater

Bob: We'd like two tickets for the 3:30 show, please.

Ticket sales: Here you go. Enjoy the movie!

[Inside the theater]

Bob: Would you mind moving over one, so my friend and I can sit together?

Woman: No, not at all.

Bob: Thank you so much!

20. ما هي الأشياء التي أنت جيد في القيام بها؟ – WHAT ARE YOU GOOD AT DOING?

(mā hy āl'šyā' ālty 'nt ğyd fy ālqyām bhā؟)

ساندرا: إذًا ... ماذا يجب أن نفعل؟

sāndrā: 'dā ... mādā yğb 'n nf'l؟

جولي: حسنًا، أحب ممارسة الفنون والحرف، فأنا جيدة جدًا في الرسم. ما رأيك؟

ğwly: ḥsnā، 'ḥb mmārsة ālfnwn wālḥrf، f'nā ğydة ğdā fy ālrsm. mā r'yk؟

ساندرا: هممم ... ماذا عن لعب لعبة لوحية؟ سيكون هذا ممتعًا أكثر.

sāndrā: hmmm ... mādā 'n l'b l'bة lwḥy؟ة sykwn hdā mmt'ā 'ktr.

جولي: حسنًا. هيا نلعب سكرابل! أنا ممتازة في التهجئة!

ğwly: ḥsnā. hyā nl'b skrābl! 'nā mmtāzة fy ālthğئة!

ساندرا: لِنرى ذلك!

sāndrā: lnrى dlk!

What Are You Good At Doing?

Sandra: So ... what should we do?

Julie: Well, I like to do arts and crafts, and I'm really good at drawing. What do you think?

Sandra: Hmm ... how about playing a board game? That would be more fun.

Julie: Ok. Let's play Scrabble! I'm really good at spelling, too!

Sandra: Oh, yeah? We'll see about that!

21. ما هي الرياضة المفضلة لديك؟ – What Is Your Favorite Sport?

(mā hy ālryāḍẗ ālmfḍlẗ ldykʕ)

فيل: متى تبدأ مباراة كرة القدم؟ اعتقدت أنها تبدأ عند الظهر.
fyl: mtى tbdʾ mbārāẗ krẗ ālqdmʕ āʿtqdt ʾnhā tbdʾ ʿnd ālẓhr.

جاك: أظن أننا مخطئان في الوقت. أوه، حسنًا ... على أي حال كرة القدم ليست رياضتي المفضلة. أنا أفضل كرة السلة.
ğāk: ʾẓn ʾnnā mẖṭئān fy ālwqt. ʾwh، ḥsnā̃ ... ʿlʾ ʾy ḥāl krẗ ālqdm lyst ryāḍty ālmfḍlʾ .ẗnā ʾfḍl krẗ ālslẗ.

فيل: أوه حقا؟ اعتقدت أن رياضتك المفضلة هي التنس! أنا من أشد المعجبين بكرة السلة أيضًا.
fyl: ʾwh ḥqāʕ āʿtqdt ʾn ryāḍtk ālmfḍlẗ hy āltns! ʾnā mn ʾšd ālmʿğbyn bkrẗ ālslʾ ẗyḍā̃.

جاك: ما رأيك أن نشاهد مباراة في بعض الأحيان؟
ğāk: mā rʾyk ʾn nšāhd mbārāẗ fy bʿḍ ālʾḥyānʕ

فيل: أكيد! لِمَ لا نذهب لإطلاق بعض الأطواق الآن لأن لعبة كرة القدم لم تبدأ بعد؟
fyl: ʾkyd! lm َlā nḏhb lإṭlāq bʿḍ ālʾṭwāq ālآn lʾn lʿbẗ krẗ ālqdm lm tbdʾ bʿdʕ

جاك: فكرة ممتازة لنذهب إذًا.
ğāk: fkrẗ mmtāzẗ lnḏhb إḏā̃.

WHAT IS YOUR FAVORITE SPORT?

Phil: What time is that soccer game on? I thought it started at noon.

Jack: We must have had the wrong time. Oh, well ... soccer's not my favorite sport anyway. I much prefer basketball.

Phil: Oh, really? I thought your favorite sport was tennis! I'm a big fan of basketball, too.

Jack: How about a game sometime?

Phil: Sure thing! Why don't we go shoot some hoops now since the soccer game isn't on?

Jack: Excellent idea. Let's go.

22. Going To See A Musical – الذهاب لمشاهدة مسرحية موسيقية
(āldhāb lmšāhdة msrḥyة mwsyqyة)

شانون: يا له من أداء عظيم! شكرًا لدعوتي إلى المسرحية الموسيقية.
šānwn: yā lh mn ʾdāʾ ʿẓym! škrā̋ ldʿwty ʾlى ālmsrḥyة ālmwsyqyة.

إيلينا: أهلًا بك. أنا سعيدة أنك استمتعت بهذا العرض. كان كورو غرافي الراقصين مذهلًا. ذكرني بنفسي عندما كنت أرقص منذ سنوات عديدة.
ʾylynā: ʾhlā̋ bk. ʾnā sʿydة ʾnk āstmtʿt bhd̠ā ālʿrḍ. kān kwrw ġrāfy ālrāqṣyn md̠hlā̋. d̠krny bnfsy ʿndmā knt ʾrqṣ mnd̠ snwāt ʿdydة.

شانون: أعلم! لقد كنتِ مؤدية باليه موهوبة. هل تفتقدين الرقص؟
šānwn: ʾʿlm! lqd knt mʾd̠yة bālyh mwhwb.ة hl tftqdyn ālrqṣ?

إيلينا: أوه، هذا لطيف منك يا شانون. أفتقده في بعض الأحيان. لكنني سأظل دائمًا من المعجبين بالفنون. هذا هو السبب في أنني أحب الذهاب إلى المسرحيات الموسيقية لأنها مزيج مثالي من الرقص والأغنية والمسرح.
ʾylynā: ʾwh، hd̠ā lṭyf mnk yā šānwn. ʾftqdh fy bʿḍ ālʾḥyān. lknny sʾẓl dāʾmā̋ mn ālmʿǧbyn bālfnwn. hd̠ā hw ālsbb fy ʾnny ʾḥb āld̠hāb ʾlى ālmsrḥyāt ālmwsyqyة lʾnhā mzyǧ mt̠āly mn ālrqṣ wālʾġnyة wālmsrḥ.

شانون: أكيد! أنا سعيد أنك لا تزالين مولعة بالفن أيضًا. شكرًا لدعوتك. إنه لمن دواعي سروري دائمًا حضور حدث فني معك وتعلم شيء جديد.
šānwn: ʾkyd! ʾnā sʿyd ʾnk lā tzālyn mwlʿة bālfn ʾyḍā̋. škrā̋ ldʿwtk. ʾnh lmn dwāʿy srwry dāʾmā̋ ḥḍwr ḥdt̠ fny mʿk wtʿlm šyʾ ǧdyd.

Going To See A Musical

Shannon: What a fantastic performance! Thank you for inviting me to the musical.

Elena: You are welcome. I'm happy you enjoyed the show. The choreography of the dancers was incredible. It reminds me of when I used to dance many years ago.

Shannon: I know! You were such a talented ballerina. Do you miss dancing?

Elena: Oh, that's very kind of you, Shannon. I do miss it sometimes. But I will always be a fan of the arts. That's why I love going to musicals because it's the perfect combination of dance, song and theater.

Shannon: Absolutely! I'm glad you are still an art fan too. Thank you for the invitation. It's always a pleasure to attend an arts event with you and learn something new.

23. أخذ إجازة – TAKING A VACATION
(ʾẖḏ ʾiǧāzẗ)

جولي: لقد اشتريت لتوي تذكرة إلى مدينة نيويورك. أنا متحمسة جدًّا لرؤية المدينة!
ǧwly: lqd āštryt ltwy tḏkrẗ ʾilى mdynẗ nywywrk. ʾnā mtḥmsẗ ǧdًّā lrؤyẗ ālmdynẗ!

صوفي: عظيم جدًا! فالسفر ممتع للغاية. أحب اكتشاف أماكن جديدة وأشخاص جدد. متى ستغادرين؟
ṣwfy: ʿẓym ǧdًā! fālsfr mmtʿ llġāyẗ. ʾḥb āktšāf ʾmākn ǧdydẗ wʾšẖāṣ ǧdd. mtى stġādryn؟

جولي: الأسبوع القادم. سأركب طائرة العين الحمراء فهي أرخص ثمنًا. أتمنى أن أستطيع ان أنام على متن الطائرة.
ǧwly: ālʾsbwʿ ālqādm. sʾrkb ṭāئrẗ ālʿyn ālḥmrāʾ fhy ʾrẖṣ ṯmnًā. ʾtmnى ʾn ʾstṭyʿ ān ʾnām ʿlى mtn ālṭāئrẗ.

صوفي: كان بودّي أن أذهب معك! نيويورك تسحر الأنظار. سوف تستمتعين كثيرًا.
ṣwfy: kān bwdّy ʾn ʾḏhb mʿk! nywywrk tsḥr ālʾnẓār. swf tstmtʿyn kṯyrًā.

جولي: كان بودّي ذلك أيضًا. سأقوم بزيارة أخي الذي يعيش هناك. سوف أبقى لمدة أسبوع ومن ثم آخذ القطار إلى واشنطن العاصمة.
ǧwly: kān bwdّy ḏlk ʾyḍًā. sʾqwm bzyārẗ ʾẖy ālḏy yʿyš hnāk. swf ʾbqى lmdẗ ʾsbwʿ wmn ṯm ʾẖḏ ālqṭār ʾilى wāšnṭn ālʿāṣmẗ.

صوفي: إنها تبدو إجازة رائعة. أنا أتطلع إلى قضاء أسبوع على الشاطئ لإجازتي الصيفية. أنا أريد الاسترخاء فحسب.
ṣwfy: ʾinhā tbdw ʾiǧāzẗ rāئʿẗ. ʾnā ʾtṭlʿ ʾilى qḍāʾ ʾsbwʿ ʿlى ālšāṭئ lʾiǧāzty ālṣyfyẗ. ʾnā ʾryd ālāstrẖāʾ fḥsb.

TAKING A VACATION

Julie: I just bought a ticket to New York City. I'm so excited to see the city!

Sophie: Good for you! Traveling is so much fun. I love discovering new places and new people. When are you leaving?

Julie: Next week. I'm taking the red eye. It was cheaper. Hopefully, I'll be able to sleep on the plane.

Sophie: I wish I could go with you! New York City is a magical place. You will have so much fun.

Julie: I hope so. I'm going to visit my brother who lives there. I will stay for a week and then take the train down to Washington, DC

Sophie: That sounds like a great vacation. I'm looking forward to a week at the beach for my summer vacation. I just want to relax.

24. في متجر الحيوانات – AT THE PET STORE

(fy mtğr ālḥywānāt)

كوني: إنها لقطة رائعة! ما رأيك؟

kwny: !nhā lqṭ‎ۃ rāئ‎ʿۃ! mā rʾyk؟

غاري: أعتقد أنه من الأفضل أن أحصل على كلب. الكلاب أكثر ولاء من القطط. القطط كائنات كسولة جدًا.

ġāry: ʾʿtqd ʾnh mn ālʾfḍl ʾn ʾḥṣl ʿlى klb. ālklāb ʾkṯr wlāʾ mn ālqṭṭ. ālqṭṭ kāئnāt kswlۃ ğdًā.

كوني: نعم، لكنهم يحتاجون إلى الكثير من الرعاية والاهتمام! هل ستكون على استعداد للاعتناء بها كل يوم؟ وتنظيفها باستمرار؟

kwny: nʿm ، lknhm yḥtāğwn !lى ālkṯyr mn ālrʿāyۃ wālāhtmām! hl stkwn ʿlى āstʿdād llāʿtnāʾ bhā kl ywm؟ wtnẓyfhā bāstmrār؟

غاري: أحسنت. ماذا عن عصفور؟ أو سمكة؟

ġāry: ʾḥsnt. māḏā ʿn ʿṣfwrʾ ؟w smk؟ۃ

كوني: سيكون على أن أدفع الكثير من الأموال لشراء قفص أو حوض للأسماك. وأنا بصراحة لا أعرف كيف أعتني بالعصافير أو الأسماك!

kwny: sykwn ʿly ʾn ʾdfʿ ālkṯyr mn ālʾmwāl lšrāʾ qfṣ ʾw ḥwḍ llʾsmāk. wʾnā bṣrāḥۃ lā ʾʿrf kyf ʾʿtny bālʿṣāfyr ʾw ālʾsmāk!

غاري: حسنًا، من الواضح أننا لسنا مستعدين للحصول على حيوان الآن.

ġāry: ḥsnًā، mn ālwāḍḥ ʾnnā lsnā mstʿdyn llḥṣwl ʿlى ḥywān ālʾn.

كوني: هههههههه ... نعم، أنت محق. هيّا بنا نحصل على بعض الطعام ونتحدث عن ذلك.

kwny: hhhhhhhh ... nʿm، ʾnt mḥq. hyّā bnā nḥṣl ʿlى bʿḍ ālṭʿām wntḥdṯ ʿn ḏlk.

AT THE PET STORE

Connie: What a beautiful cat! What do you think?

Gary: I think I'd rather get a dog. Dogs are more loyal than cats. Cats are just lazy.

Connie: Yes, but they need so much attention! Would you be willing to walk it every single day? And clean up after it?

Gary: Hmm. Good point. What about a bird? Or a fish?

Connie: We'd have to invest a lot of money in a cage or a fish tank. And I honestly don't know how to take care of a bird or a fish!

Gary: Well, we're obviously not ready to get a pet yet.

Connie: Haha... Yeah, you're right. Let's get some food and talk about it.

25. التعبير عن رأيك – EXPRESSING YOUR OPINION
(ālt‘byr ‘n rأyk)

جايك: أين نذهب في إجازة هذا العام؟ نحن بحاجة إلى أن نقرر قريبًا.
ğāyk: أyn nḏhb fy إğāzة hḏā āl‘ām؟ nḥn bḥāğإ ةlأ ىn nqrr qrybًā.

ميليسا: حسنًا, أود أن أذهب إلى مكان دافئ. ما رأيك بالشاطئ؟ أو يمكننا استئجار مقصورة على البحيرة.
mylysā: ḥsnًā, أwd أn أḏhb إlى mkān dāf.ئ mā rأyk bālšāṭأ ؟ئw ymknnā āstئğār mqṣwrة ‘lى ālbḥyrة.

جايك: أتريدين الذهاب إلى الشاطئ مرة أخرى؟ أريد أن أتزلج في هذا الشتاء. يمكننا أن نتفاهم ونسافر إلى جبال روكي في ولاية كولورادو في أبريل المقبل؟ هناك منتجعات رائعة للتزلج على الجليد هناك.
ğāyk: أtrydyn ālḏhāb إlى ālšāṭئ mrأ ةẖrأ ؟ىryd أn أtzlğ fy hḏā ālštā’. ymknnā أn ntfāhm wnsāfr إlى ğbāl rwky fy wlāyة kwlwrādw fy أbryl ālmqbl؟ hnāk mntğ‘āt rāئ‘ة lltzlğ ‘lى ālğlyd hnāk.

ميليسا: أوه, صحيح فنحن لم نذهب إلى كولورادو من قبل! لكنّي لا أعرف ما إذا سيكون يوما مشمسًا ودافئًا عندها. أحتاج إلى القيام بالبحث أولًا. سيساعدني ذلك في اتخاذ القرار.
mylysā: أwh, ṣḥyḥ fnḥn lm nḏhb إlى kwlwrādw mn qbl! lknّy lā أ‘rf mā إḏā sykwn ywmā mšmsًā wdāfئًā ‘ndhā. أḥtāğ إlى ālqyām bālbḥṯ أwlًā. sysā‘dny ḏlk fy ātẖāḏ ālqrār.

EXPRESSING YOUR OPINION

Jake: Where should we take a vacation this year? We need to decide soon.

Melissa: Well, I'd like to go somewhere warm. How about the beach? Or we could rent a cabin on the lake.

Jake: You want to go to the beach, again? I want to ski this winter. We can compromise and travel to the Rocky Mountains in Colorado next April? There are beautiful ski resorts there.

Melissa: Oh, we've never been to Colorado before! But I don't know if it will be sunny and warm then. I need to do some research first. That will help me make a decision.

26. الهوايات – HOBBIES
(ālhwāyāt)

ريان: أنا فرح جدًا هذا الأسبوع لأن اختبارات منتصف الفصل قد انتهت.

ryān: ỉnā frḥ ğdā̃ hḏā ālỉsbwʿ lỉn āḫtbārāt mntṣf ālfṣl qd ānth t.

تايلر: أنا مثلك. فأنا أتطلع إلى الاسترخاء في الجبال في نهاية هذا الأسبوع. لقد خططت لجولة في الغابة. أيضًا، إذا كان الطقس جيدًا، سأذهب للتجديف في النهر.

tāylr: ỉnā mṯlk. fỉnā ỉtṭlʿ ỉlى ālāstrḫāʾ fy ālğbāl fy nhāyة hḏā ālỉsbwʿ. lqd ḫṭṭt lğwlة fy ālġābỉ .ةyḍā، ỉḏā kān ālṭqs ğydā̃، sỉḏhb lltğdyf fy ālnhr.

ريان: أوه ،ممتع! أنا ذاهب إلى كولورادو. أنا آخذ الكاميرا لأن الخريف سوف يأتي بسرعة. الأوراق تأخذ بالفعل جميع أطياف اللون الأحمر والبرتقالي. سيكون ذلك ساحرًا.

ryān: ỉwh ،mmtʿ! ỉnā ḏāhb ỉlى kwlwrādw. ỉnā ʾāḫḏ ālkāmyrā lỉn ālḫryf swf yỉty bsrʿ.ة ālỉwrāq tỉḫḏ bālfʿl ğmyʿ ỉṭyāf āllwn ālỉḥmr wālbrtqāly. sykwn ḏlk sāḥrā̃.

تايلر: في المرة القادمة عندما تذهب إلى هناك، سوف أكون معك. لقد سمعت أن كولورادو مكان رائع للتجديف.

tāylr: fy ālmrة ālqādmة ʿndmā tḏhb ỉlى hnāk، swf ỉkwn mʿk. lqd smʿt ỉn kwlwrādw mkān rāئʿ lltğdyf.

HOBBIES

Ryan: I'm so happy this week of midterm exams is finished.

Tyler: Same here. I'm looking forward to relaxing in the mountains this weekend. I've planned a nice little hike in the woods. Also, if the weather is good, I'm going to go canoeing down the river.

Ryan: Oh, how fun! I'm going to Colorado. I'm taking my camera because fall is coming fast. The leaves are already turning all shades of red and orange. It will be awesome.

Tyler: Next time you go there, I'll join you. I've heard Colorado is a great place to go canoeing.

27. حفلة الزواج – THE WEDDING
(ḥflẗ ālzwāǧ)

أنجليكا: ألا تبدو العروس جميلة في ثوب الزفاف هذا؟
ỉnǧlykā: ỉlā tbdw āl'rws ǧmylẗ fy ṯwb ālzfāf hḏā؟

ماريا: نعم. إنها تبدو رائعة. والعريس رومنسي أيضًا.
māryā: n'm. ỉnhā tbdw rāỷʿ.ẗ wāl'rys rwmnsy ỉyḍā.

لقد سمعت قصة ارتباطهما! لقد تقدم لها في عشاء على ضوء الشموع في براغ. كان ذلك حين ذهابهم للجامعة.
lqd smʿt qṣẗ ārtbāṭhmā! lqd tqdm lhā fy ʿšāʾ ʿly ḍwʾ ālšmwʿ fy brāġ. kān ḏlk ḥyn ḏhābhm llǧāmʿẗ.

انجليكا: صحيح؟ رائع. وشهر العسل! يالها من فكرة رائعة! معظم الناس يذهبون إلى الشاطئ لمدة أسبوع بعد كتابة القران. أعتقد أن هذه الفكرة مملة للغاية. بدلًا من ذلك، هما يخططان للذهاب إلى كاليفورنيا والتجول على الساحل باستعمال دراجتيهما النارية.
ānǧlykā: ṣḥyḥ؟ rāỷʿ. wšhr ālʿsl! yālhā mn fkrẗ rāỷʿẗ! mʿẓm ālnās yḏhbwn ỉly ālšāṭỷ lmdẗ ỉsbwʿ bʿd ktābẗ ālqrān. ỉʿtqd ỉn hḏh ālfkrẗ mmlẗ llġāy.ẗ bdlā mn ḏlk، hmā yḫṭṭān llḏhāb ỉly kālyfwrnyā wāltǧwl ʿly ālsāḥl bāstʿmāl drāǧtyhmā ālnāryẗ.

ماريا: هل هذ صحيح؟ يا لها من فكرة رائعة. هذا هو أفضل زفاف رأته عيني.
māryā: hl hḏ ṣḥyḥ؟ yā lhā mn fkrẗ rāỷʿ.ẗ hḏā hw ỉfḍl zfāf rỉth ʿyny.

THE WEDDING

Angelica: Doesn't the bride look beautiful in that wedding dress?

Maria: Yes. She looks amazing. And the groom is such a romantic.

I just heard the story of how they got engaged! He proposed to her during a candlelight dinner in Prague. That was where they went to school.

Angelica: Oh yea? Wonderful. And the honeymoon! What a great idea! Most people just go to the beach for a week after they tie the knot. I think that's such a boring idea. Instead, they plan on going to California and cruising the coast on their motorcycle.

Maria: Really! What a fantastic idea. This is by far the best wedding I've ever been to in my life!

28. تقديم النصيحة – GIVING ADVICE
(tqdym ālnṣyḥẗ)

ليلى: أشكرك على مقابلتي في ساعة الغداء. أنا أحترم ذلك.
lylỉ :ىškrk ʿlى mqāblty fy sāʿẗ ālġdā'. ỉnā ỉḥtrm ḏlk.

مونيكا: لا مشكلة. أنا سعيدة للمساعدة. ماذا يحدث؟
mwnykā: lā mšklỉ .ẗnā sʿydẗ llmsāʿd.ẗ māḏā yḥdṯ؟

ليلى: يا إلهي، كالمعتاد يجب أن أتخذ قراري قريبًا ... هل يجب أن أتولى هذه الوظيفة الجديدة؟ أو هل يجب أن أتمسك بوظيفتي الحالية؟
lyl:ى yā !lhy، kālmʿtād yğb ỉn ỉtḫḏ qrāry qrybā̈ ... hl yğb ỉn ỉtwlى hḏh ālwẓyfẗ ālğdydỉ ؟ẗw hl yğb ỉn ỉtmsk bwẓyfty ālḥāly؟ẗ

مونيكا: حسنًا، أعتقد أن الوقت قد حان للتجديد، أليس كذلك؟ إنهم يدفعون لك في وقت متأخر وأنتِ غير سعيدة. هذه أكثر من أسباب كافية لإنهاء عملك.
mwnykā: ḥsnā̈، ỉʿtqd ỉn ālwqt qd ḥān lltğdyd، ỉlys kḏlk! ؟nhm ydfʿwn lk fy wqt mtỉḫr wỉnt.ġyr sʿyd.ẗ hḏh ỉkṯr mn ỉsbāb kāfyẗ l!nhā' ʿmlk.

ليلى: هل تعتقدين ذلك حقًا؟
lyl:ى hl tʿtqdyn ḏlk ḥqā̈؟

مونيكا: أعرف ذلك. لقد كنت أستمع إلى شكواك منذ أكثر من عام. ثقي بي. خذي الوظيفة. ماذا لديكِ لتخسريه؟
mwnykā: ỉʿrf ḏlk. lqd knt ỉstmʿ !lى škwāk mnḏ ỉkṯr mn ʿām. ṯqy by. ḫḏy ālwẓyf.ẗ māḏā ldyk.ltḫsryh؟

ليلى: صحيح, لقد أقنعتِني. أنتِ دائمًا تعطيني أفضل نصيحة.
lyl:ى ṣḥyḥ, lqd ỉqnʿtny. ỉnt.dāئmā̈ tʿṭyny ỉfḍl nṣyḥẗ.

GIVING ADVICE

Layla: Thanks for meeting with me during your lunch hour. I appreciate it.

Monica: No problem. I'm happy to help. What's happening?

Layla: Oh, you know, the usual. I have to decide soon... Should I take this new job? Or do I stick with my current one?

Monica: Well, I think it's time for a change, don't you? They pay you late and you are unhappy. That's more than enough reasons to quit your job.

Layla: Do you really think so?

Monica: I know so. And I've been listening to you complain for over a year now. Trust me. Take the job. What do you have to lose?

Layla: Ok, you convinced me. You have always given me the best advice.

29. تعليم الاطفال – TEACHING CHILDREN
(tʿlym ālāṭfāl)

سام: مرحبًا جاك، كيف كان يومك؟

sām: mrḥbā̃ ǧāk، kyf kān ywmk؟

جاك: مرحبًا سام، أين كنتِ؟ لقد كنت أبحث عنكِ.

ǧāk: mrḥbā̃ sām، ỉyn knt؟ lqd knt ỉbḥṯ ʿnk.

سام: لن تصدق التجربة الرائعة التي مررت بها للتو. لقد قضيت اليوم كله مع الكثير من الأطفال!

sām: ln tṣdq āltǧrbẗ ālrāỷʿẗ ālty mrrt bhā lltw. lqd qḍyt ālywm klh mʿ ālkṯyr mn ālỉṭfāl!

جاك: يبدو ذلك ممتعًا. أخبريني أكثر عن ذلك.

ǧāk: ybdw ḏlk mmtʿā̃. ỉḫbryny ỉkṯr ʿn ḏlk.

سام: نعم، لقد كان وقتًا رائعًا ... ولكنه كان مرهقًا للغاية! لم أكن أدرك أن الأطفال لديهم الكثير من الطاقة.

sām: nʿm، lqd kān wqtā̃ rāỷʿā̃ ... wlknh kān mrhqā̃ llġāyẗ! lm ỉkn ỉdrk ỉn ālỉṭfāl ldyhm ālkṯyr mn ālṭāqẗ.

جاك: وأين التقيتِ بكل هؤلاء الأطفال؟

ǧāk: wỉyn āltqyt bkl hw̉lā' ālỉṭfāl؟

سام: في المدرسة الابتدائية في شيكاغو. أتيحت لي الفرصة لزيارة بعض دروسهم في الصباح. بعد ذلك علمتهم بعض قواعد الإنجليزية مع ألعاب الكلمات في فترة ما بعد الظهر.

sām: fy ālmdrsẗ ālābtdāỷyẗ fy šykāġw. ỉtyḥt ly ālfrṣẗ lzyārẗ bʿḍ drwshm fy ālṣbāḥ. bʿd ḏlk ʿlmthm bʿḍ qwāʿd ālỉnǧlyzyẗ mʿ ỉlʿāb ālklmāt fy ftrẗ mā bʿd ālẓhr.

جاك: أنا متأكد أن الإنجليزية كانت صعبة للغاية بالنسبة لهم.
ğāk: انā mtاkd ان ālإnğlyzyة kānt ṣʿbة llġāyة bālnsbة lhm.

سام: من المدهش أن الجميع كانوا متلهفين للتعلم. بصراحة، لقد أعجبوني.
sām: mn ālmdhš ان ālğmyʿ kānwā mtlhfyn lltʿlm. bṣrāḥ،ة lqd
اʿğbwny.

جاك: هذا رائع. وكيف قمتِ بتعليمهم؟
ğāk: hḏā rāئʿ. wkyf qmtِ btʿlymhm؟

سام: يحب الأطفال تكرار الأشياء بصوت عال! في بعض الأحيان صرخت بالجمل، وصاحوا في وجهي. همست، وهمسوا مرة أخرى. لقد شعرت بالكثير من المرح!
sām: yḥb ālاṭfāl tkrār ālاšyāʾ bṣwt ʿāl! fy bʿḍ ālاḥyān ṣrẖt bālğml، wṣāḥwā fy wğhy. hmst، whmswā mrاةẖr.ى lqd šʿrt bālktẖyr mn ālmrḥ!

جاك: تعرفين، عندما كنت طالبًا أجنبيًا، لم يكن لدينا دروس في اللغة الإنجليزية من هذا القبيل. يجعلني أشعر بالسعادة أن الأطفال خاضوا مثل هذه التجربة الرائعة.
ğāk: tʿrfyn، ʿndmā knt ṭālbًā اğnbyًā، lm ykn ldynā drws fy āllġة ālإnğlyzyة mn hḏā ālqbyl. yğʿlny اšʿr bālsʿādا ةn ālاṭfāl ẖāḍwā mtẖl hḏh āltğrbة ālrāئʿة.

TEACHING CHILDREN

Sam: Hi Jack, how was your day?

Jack: Hi Sam, where have you been? I've been looking for you.

Sam: You won't believe the interesting experience I just had. I spent the whole day with a ton of children!

Jack: That sounds like fun. Tell me more.

Sam: Yes, it was a great time... but it was so exhausting! I didn't realize that kids have so much energy.

Jack: Where did you meet all these kids?

Sam: At the elementary school in Chicago. I had an opportunity to visit some of their classes in the morning. After that I taught them some basic English with word games in the afternoon.

Jack: I'm sure English was probably very difficult for them.

Sam: Surprisingly, they were all very eager to learn. Honestly, I was impressed.

Jack: That's great. What did you end up teaching them?

Sam: The kids love to repeat things out loud! Sometimes I yelled out the sentences, and they yelled back at me. I whispered, and they whispered back. It was so much fun!

Jack: You know, when I was a foreign exchange student, we never had English lessons like that. It makes me happy the children had such a wonderful experience.

30. متعة لعب كرة المضرب – FUN WITH TENNIS
(mtʿꞨ lʿb krꞨ ālmḍrb)

ألما: سيباستيان، هل يمكن أن تعلمني كيف أمسك بالمضرب؟
ỉlmā: sybāstyān، hl ymkn ỉn tʿlmny kyf ỉmsk bālmḍrb؟

سيباستيان: بالتأكيد ألما، مثلما نصافح تمامًا. امسكي يدك كما لو أنكِ تصافحين يدي ...
sybāstyān: bāltỉkyd ỉlmā، mṯlmā nṣāfḥ tmāmā̋. āmsky ydk kmā lw ỉnk.tṣāfḥyn ydy ...

ألما: فقط مثل هذا؟
ỉlmā: fqṭ mṯl hḏā؟

سيباستيان: نعم, مثل ذلك تمام. و الآن امسكي المضرب في يدك هكذا.
sybāstyān: nʿm, mṯl ḏlk tmām. w ālỉn āmsky ālmḍrb fy ydk hkḏā.

ألما: الآن أنا مستعدة لضرب الكرة كالمحترفين!
ỉlmā: ālỉn ỉnā mstʿdꞨ lḍrb ālkrꞨ kālmḥtrfyn!

سيباستيان: هههههه، تقريبًا! تذكري ما أخبرتك به, لا يوجد سوى نوعين من التقلبات، الاستدارة الأمامية والخلفية.
sybāstyān: hhhhhh، tqrybā̋! tḏkry mā ỉẖbrtk bh, lā ywǧd swى nwʿyn mn āltqlbāt، ālāstdārꞨ ālỉmāmyꞨ wālẖlfyꞨ.

ألما: جيد, أنا أتذكر. لقد قلت أن ضرب استدارة أمامية، بدءاً من يميني، هو كضرب كرة طاولة.
ỉlmā: ǧyd,ỉ nā ỉtḏkr. lqd qlt ỉn ḍrb āstdārỉ Ꞩmāmy،Ꞩ bdʾā̋mn ymyny، hw kḍrb krꞨ ṭāwlꞨ.

سيباستيان: هذا صحيح. جربي الآن. هل أنتِ جاهزة؟ اضربي هذه!
sybāstyān: hḏā ṣḥyḥ. ğrby ālʾn. hl ʾntِ ğāhzة؟ āḍrby hḏh!

ألما: معذرة, فقد فاتني ذلك تمامًا!
ʾlmā: mʿḏr,ة fqd fātny ḏlk tmāmًā!

سيباستيان: لا مشكلة، حاولي مرة أخرى.
sybāstyān: lā mškl،ة ḥāwly mrʾ ةḫrى.

ألما: أوه، أرى. دعني أحاول مجددًا...
ʾlmā: ʾwh، ʾr.ى dʿny ʾḥāwl mğddًā...

سيباستيان: إليكِ كرة أخرى ... واو! لقد ضربتها فوق السور! أنتِ فتاة قوية للغاية.
sybāstyān: ʾlykِ krʾ ةḫrى ... wāw! lqd ḍrbthā fwq ālswr! ʾntِ ftāة qwyة llġāyة.

ألما: ههه, أعتقد أنني بحاجة إلى المزيد من الممارسة.
ʾlmā: hhhh,ʾ ʿtqd ʾnny bḥāğ ةʾlى ālmzyd mn ālmmārsة.

FUN WITH TENNIS

Alma: Sebastian, could you show me how to hold the racket?

Sebastian: Sure Alma, it's just like when we shake hands. Hold your hand out as if you were about to shake my hand...

Alma: Just like this?

Sebastian: Yes, just like that. Now, put the racket in your hand, like this.

Alma: Now I'm ready to hit the ball like a professional!

Sebastian: Haha, almost! Remember what I told you. There are only two types of swings, the forehand and the backhand.

Alma: Ok, I remember. You said hitting a forehand, starting on my right, is like hitting a ping pong ball.

Sebastian: That's right. Give it a try now. Are you ready? Hit this!

Alma: Oops! I completely missed it!

Sebastian: That's alright, try again.

Alma: Oh, I see. Let me try again...

Sebastian: Here comes another ball... Wow! You hit it over the fence! You're a very powerful lady.

Alma: Haha. I guess I need to practice more!

31. العيش في كاليفورنيا – Living In California
(āl'yš fy kālyfwrnyā)

جيسيكا: إن الجو بارد جدًّا هذا الصباح.
ğysykā: !n ālğw bārd ğdā̃ hḏā ālṣbāḥ.

تاتيانا: بالتأكيد. في وقت مبكر من هذا الصباح، اضطررت لأن أرش الزجاج الأمامي لسيارتي لأنها كانت مغطاة بالثلج.
tātyānā: bāltˡkyd. fy wqt mbkr mn hḏā ālṣbāḥ، āḍṭrrt lˡn ˡrš ālzğāğ ālˡmāmy lsyārty lˡnhā kānt mġṭāۃ bālṯlğ.

جيسيكا: لم أكن لأفكر أبدًا أن هذا البرد يمكن أن يكون في أوائل ديسمبر، خاصة في كاليفورنيا.
ğysykā: lm ˡkn lˡfkr ˡbdā̃ ˡn hḏā ālbrd ymkn ˡn ykwn fy ˡwāئl dysmbr، ḫāṣۃ fy kālyfwrnyā.

تاتيانا: أعرف. كانت درجة الحرارة 40 درجة فهرنهايت عندما استيقظت هذا الصباح. كنت أتجمد من البرد حالما نزلت من السرير. الطقس البارد لم يكن بالتأكيد مفاجأة ظريفة.
tātyānā: ˡ'rf. kānt drğۃ ālḥrār40 ۃ drğۃ fhrnhāyt 'ndmā āstyqẓt hḏā ālṣbāḥ. knt ˡtğmd mn ālbrd ḥālmā nzlt mn ālsryr. ālṭqs ālbārd lm ykn bāltˡkyd mfāğۃˡ ẓryfۃ.

جيسيكا: لا أتذكر متى كان الطقس بهذه البرودة في شهر ديسمبر.
ğysykā: lā ˡtḏkr mtى kān ālṭqs bhḏh ālbrwdۃ fy šhr dysmbr.

تاتيانا: ما أتعس من ذلك هو أنها سوف تمطر بعد ظهر اليوم. سيكون الجو باردًا ورطبًا!
tātyānā: mā ˡt's mn ḏlk hw ˡnhā swf tmṭr b'd ẓhr ālywm. sykwn ālğw bārdā̃ wrṭbā̃!

جيسيكا: ماذا؟! سوف تمطر بعد ظهر هذا اليوم؟
ğysykā: māḏā؟! swf tmṭr bʿd ẓhr hḏā ālywm؟

تاتيانا: ليس فقط بعد ظهر هذا اليوم، ولكن أيضًا بقية الأسبوع. وقالوا في النشرة الجوية أن الرذاذ سيبدأ قبل الظهر مباشرة، وبعد ذلك سوف تمطر بشدة من الساعة الرابعة.
tātyānā: lys fqṭ bʿd ẓhr hḏā ālywm، wlkn ʾyḍā bqyة ālʾsbwʿ. wqālwā fy ālnšrة ālğwyʾ ةn ālrḏāḏ sybdʾ qbl ālẓhr mbāšr،ة wbʿd ḏlk swf tmṭr bšdة mn ālsāʿة ālrābʿة.

جيسيكا: أظن أنه ليس هناك أي شيء يشير إلى طقس جيد هذا الأسبوع؟
ğysykā: ʾẓn ʾnh lys hnāk ʾy šyʾ yšyr ʾlى ṭqs ğyd hḏā ālʾsbwʿ؟

تاتيانا: هناك فرصة ضئيلة لأن تشرق الشمس بحلول يوم السبت. ومع ذلك، سيكون يومًا ضبابيًا مصحوبًا بالرياح والأمطار قبل أن تشرق الشمس في نهاية هذا الأسبوع.
tātyānā: hnāk frṣة ḍئylة lʾn tšrq ālšms bḥlwl ywm ālsbt. wmʿ ḏlk، sykwn ywmًā ḍbābyًā mṣḥwbًā bālryāḥ wālʾmṭār qbl ʾn tšrq ālšms fy nhāyة hḏā ālʾsbwʿ.

جيسيكا: يسعدني أن تمطر على الرغم من أنني لا أحب الطقس الممطر. إن الموسم جاف للغاية حتى الآن هذه السنة.
ğysykā: ysʿdny ʾn tmṭr ʿlى ālrġm mn ʾnny lā ʾḥb ālṭqs ālmmṭr. ʾn ālmwsm ğāf llġāyة ḥtى ālʾn hḏh ālsnة.

تاتيانا: نعم، لا أستطيع أن أتذكر آخر مرة أمطرت. جيد طالما لا يوجد أي رعد أو صاعقة، يمكنني تحملها.
tātyānā: nʿm، lā ʾstṭyʿ ʾn ʾtḏkr ʾḫr mrʾ ةmṭrt. ğyd ṭālmā lā ywğd ʾy rʿd ʾw ṣāʿq،ة ymknny tḥmlhā.

جيسيكا: نادرًا ما يكون هناك رعد أو برق في كاليفورنيا.
ğysykā: nādrā̃ mā ykwn hnāk rʿd ʾw brq fy kālyfwrnyā.

تاتيانا: نحن محظوظون جدًا لأن كاليفورنيا لديها واحدة من أفضل المناخات الجوية في أمريكا.
tātyānā: nḥn mḥẓwẓwn ğdā̃ lʾn kālyfwrnyā ldyhā wāḥdẗ mn ʾfḍl ālmnāẖāt ālğwyẗ fy ʾmrykā.

جيسيكا: أنت محقة، هناك أماكن أسوأ يمكن أن نعيش بها. حسنًا، بدأ الدرس الآن، أراكِ لاحقًا.
ğysykā: ʾnt mḥq،ẗ hnāk ʾmākn ʾswʾ ymkn ʾn nʿyš bhā. ḥsnā̃، bdʾ āldrs ālʾn، ʾrākِ lāḥqā̃.

تاتيانا: أراكِ لاحقًا.
tātyānā: ʾrākِ lāḥqā̃.

Living In California

Jessica: It is so chilly this morning.

Tatiana: It certainly is. Early this morning I had to spray my car's windshield because it was covered with frost.

Jessica: I never would have thought it could be this cold in early December, especially in California.

Tatiana: I know. The temperature was 40 degrees Fahrenheit when I woke up this morning. I was freezing as soon as I got out of bed. The cold weather was definitely not a nice surprise.

Jessica: I can't remember when it was actually this cold in December.

Tatiana: What's worse is that it's going to rain this afternoon. It's going to be cold and wet!

Jessica: Yuck! It's going to rain this afternoon?

Tatiana: Not just this afternoon, but also the entire rest of the week. The news said that it would start to drizzle just before noon, and then it would rain really hard by four o'clock.

Jessica: I'm guessing there's no sign of better weather this week?

Tatiana: There is a slim chance of sunshine by Saturday. However, it will be foggy, windy, and rainy before the sun comes out this weekend.

Jessica: I am glad that it rains even though I do not like rainy weather. We have a very dry season so far this year.

Tatiana: Yes, I can hardly remember when it rained last time. Well, as long as there is no thunder or lightning, I can stand it.

Jessica: We rarely have thunder or lightning in California.

Tatiana: We are very lucky that California has one of the best weather conditions in America.

Jessica: You are right, there are worse places we could be living. Alright, class is starting right now so I'll see you later.

Tatiana: See you later.

32. الطهي – Baking
(ālṭhy)

تشيلسي: أمي، ماذا تطهين؟ رائحته جيدة جدًّا.
tšylsy: ꞌmy، mādā tṭhyn؟ rāئḥth ğydة ğdًّā.

السيدة كيلي: أنا أطهي الكعك. هذه هي كعكة الجزر التي تحبينها.
ālsydة kyly: ꞌnā ꞌṭhy ālkʿk. hdh hy kʿkة ālğzr ālty tḥbynhā.

تشيلسي: تبدو شهية. وأرى بعض المافن هناك أيضًا. لقد كنت منشغلة، أليس كذلك؟
tšylsy: tbdw šhy.ة wꞌrى bʿḍ ālmāfn hnāk ꞌyḍًā. lqd knt mnšġlة، ꞌlys kdlk؟

السيدة كيلي: نعم. دونوفان يجب أن يأخذ البعض إلى حفلة عيد ميلاد غدًا. لذلك، هذا المافن هو له فقط. لا تأكليهم.
ālsydة kyly: nʿm. dwnwfān yğb ꞌn yꞌḫd ālbʿḍ ꞌlى ḥflة ʿyd mylād ġdًā. ldlk، hdā ālmāfn hw lh fqṭ. lā tꞌklyhm.

تشيلسي: هل يمكنني الحصول على قطعة من كعك الجزر؟ أريد أن أستمتع بحياتي الآن.
tšylsy: hl ymknny ālḥṣwl ʿlى qṭʿة mn kʿk ālğzrꞌ ؟ryd ꞌn ꞌstmtʿ bḥyāty ālꞌn.

السيدة كيلي: ألا تريدين الانتظار حتى بعد العشاء؟
ālsydة kyly: ꞌlā trydyn ālāntẓār ḥtى bʿd ālʿšāʾ؟

تشيلسي: الكعكة تناديني، "تشيلسي، أرجوكِ التهميني." لا، لا أريد الانتظار. أمي هل يمكنني؟
tšylsy: ālkʿkة tnādyny، "tšylsy، ꞌrğwkِ ālthmyny." lā، lā ꞌryd ālāntẓār. ꞌmy hl ymknny؟

السيدة كيلي: هههههه ... حسنًا، تفضلي.
ālsydẗ kyly: hhhhhh ... ḥsnā̱، tfḍly.

تشيلسي: إذًا ما هو العشاء لليلة؟
tšylsy: !ḏā̱ mā hw ālʿšāʾ llyl؟ẗ

السيدة كيلي: سأصنع لحم بقر مشوي وكريمة من شوربة الفطر.
ālsydẗ kyly: sʾṣnʿ lḥm bqr mšwy wkrymẗ mn šwrbẗ ālfṭr.

تشيلسي: لقد مر وقت طويل منذ أن طهوت كريمة شوربة الفطر. هل تحتاجين لأية مساعدة يا أمي؟
tšylsy: lqd mr wqt ṭwyl mnḏ ʾn ṭhwt krymẗ šwrbẗ ālfṭr. hl tḥtāǧyn lʾyẗ msāʿdẗ yā ʾmy؟

السيدة كيلي: لا، قومي بواجبك المنزلي واتركي الطهي لي.
ālsydẗ kyly: lā، qwmy bwāǧbk ālmnzly wātrky ālṭhy ly.

تشيلسي: شكرًا جزيلًا يا أمي. ناديني عندما يكون العشاء جاهزًا. أنا لا أريد أن أتأخر عن لحم البقر المشوي، وكريمة شوربة الفطر، وكعك الجزر والمافن.
tšylsy: škrā̱ ǧzylā̱ yā ʾmy. nādyny ʿndmā ykwn ālʿšāʾ ǧāhzā̱. ʾnā lā ʾryd ʾn ʾtʾḫr ʿn lḥm ālbqr ālmšwy، wkrymẗ šwrbẗ ālfṭr، wkʿk ālǧzr wālmāfn.

السيدة كيلي: المافن لدونوفان. لا تلمسيهم!
ālsydẗ kyly: ālmāfn ldwnwfān. lā tlmsyhm!

تشيلسي: أعرف يا أمي. أنا فقط أمزح.
tšylsy: ʾʿrf yā ʾmy. ʾnā fqṭ ʾmzḥ.

BAKING

Chelsea: Mom, what are you cooking? It smells so good.

Mrs. Kelly: I am baking cakes. This is your favorite carrot cake.

Chelsea: It looks scrumptious. And I see muffins some over there too. You have been busy, haven't you?

Mrs. Kelly: Yes. Donovan has to take some to a birthday party tomorrow. So, those muffins are just for him. Don't eat them.

Chelsea: Can I have a piece of carrot cake? I want to enjoy life right now.

Mrs. Kelly: You don't want to wait until after dinner?

Chelsea: The cake is calling my name, "Chelsea, eat me... eat me..." No, I don't want to wait. Can I, mom?

Mrs. Kelly: Ha ha... Ok, go ahead.

Chelsea: Yum! So, what's for dinner tonight?

Mrs. Kelly: I will make roast beef and cream of mushroom soup.

Chelsea: It has been a long time since you made cream of mushroom soup. Do you need any help, mom?

Mrs. Kelly: No, go do your homework and leave the cooking to me.

Chelsea: Thanks, mom. Call me whenever dinner is ready. I do not want to be late for roast beef, cream of mushroom soup, carrot cake and muffins.

Mrs. Kelly: The muffins are for Donovan. Do not touch them!

Chelsea: I know, mom. I'm just kidding.

33. مساعدة عبر الهاتف – Help Over The Phone
(msāʿdẗ ʿbr ālhātf)

جيجي: شكرًا لك على الاتصال بمركز الترفيه الرياضي. كيف يمكنني مساعدتك؟

ğyğy: škrā lk ʿlى ālātṣāl bmrkz āltrfyh ālryāḍy. kyf ymknny msāʿdtk؟

كوليت: لقد اشتريت دراجة تمرين من متجرك منذ بضعة أشهر , وأنا أواجه مشاكلًا معها. لقد توقفت عن العمل وأنا بحاجة إلى إصلاحها.
kwlyt: lqd āštryt drāğẗ tmryn mn mtğrk mnḏ bḍʿẗ ỉšhr، wỉnā ỉwāğh mšāklā mʿhā. lqd twqft ʿn ālʿml wỉnā bḥāğẗ ỉlى ỉṣlāḥhā.

جيجي: سأحولك إلى قسم الخدمات. لحظة واحدة من فضلك.
ğyğy: sỉḥwlk ỉlى qsm ālḫdmāt. lḥẓẗ wāḥdẗ mn fḍlk.

أنجيلا: قسم الخدمات، هنا أنجيلا. كيف يمكنني مساعدتك؟
ỉnğylā: qsm ālḫdmāt، hnā ỉnğylā. kyf ymknny msāʿdtk؟

كوليت: اشتريت دراجة تمرين من المركز الرياضي العام الماضي، وتحتاج إلى إصلاح.
kwlyt: āštryt drāğẗ tmryn mn ālmrkz ālryāḍy ālʿām ālmāḍy، wtḥtāğ ỉlى ỉṣlāḥ.

أنجيلا: ما هي المشكلة؟

ỉnğylā: mā hy ālmšklẗ؟

كوليت: أنا لا أدري ما حدث، لكن شاشة الكمبيوتر سوداء ولا تشتغل بعد الآن.
kwlyt: ỉnā lā ỉdry mā ḥdṯ، lkn šāšẗ ālkmbywtr swdāʾ wlā tštġl bʿd ālỉn.

أنجيلا: هل حاولت الضغط على زر "شغل"؟

ỉnğylā: hl ḥāwlt ālḍġṭ ʿlى zr "šġl"؟

كوليت: نعم ولا شيء يشتغل.

kwlyt: nʿm wlā šyʾ yštġl.

أنجيلا: ما هو نوع الدراجة الخاصة بك؟

ỉnğylā: mā hw nwʿ āldrāğة ālẖāṣة bk؟

كوليت: إنها عبارة عن Skull Crusher 420Z، إنها واحدة ذات سلة رائعة في المقدمة.

kwlyt: ḭnhā ʿbārة ʿn Skull Crusher 420Z، ḭnhā wāḥdة ḏāt slة rāỷʿة fy ālmqdmة.

أنجيلا: يمكنني إرسال تقني فني لإلقاء نظرة على دراجتك. سيكلف ذلك 5000 دولار للعمالة. أيضًا، إذا كان علينا استبدال أي أجزاء، ستكون هناك تكاليف إضافية. هل اتفقنا؟

ỉnğylā: ymknny ḭrsāl tqny fny lḭlqāʾ nẓrة ʿlى drāğtk. syklf ḏlk 5000 dwlār llʿmālẗ. ỉyḍًā، ḭḏā kān ʿlynā āstbdāl ỉy ỉğzāʾ، stkwn hnāk tkālyf ḭḍāfyة. hl ātfqnā؟

كوليت: هذا مكلف للغاية. أليست تكاليف الإصلاح يشملها الضمان؟

kwlyt: hḏā mklf llġāyẗ. ỉlyst tkālyf ālḭṣlāḥ yšmlhā ālḍmān؟

أنجيلا: متى اشتريت دراجتك؟

ỉnğylā: mtى āštryt drāğtk؟

كوليت: منذ حوالي 3 أشهر.

kwlyt: mnḏ ḥwāly 3 ỉšhr.

أنجيلا: أنا آسفة. الضمان القياسي يشمل شهر واحد فقط. هل قمت بشراء ضمان إضافي عند الشراء؟

ٱngylā: ٱnā آsfة. āldmān ālqyāsy yšml šhr wāḥd fqṭ. hl qmt bšrā’ ḍmān إḍāfy ‘nd ālšrā’؟

كوليت: لا، لم أفعل. هل هناك أي خيارات أخرى إلى جانب دفع 5,000.00 دولار لعمالة الإصلاح؟

kwlyt: lā ،lm ٱfʿl. hl hnāk ٱy ẖyārāt ٱẖrإ ىاى ğānb dfʿ 5,000.00 dwlār lʿmālةālإṣlāḥ؟

أنجيلا: لا، أنا اخشى أن هذا لن يحدث.

ٱngylā: lāٱ ،nā āẖšٱ ىn hḏā ln yḥdṯ.

كوليت: تبًا

kwlyt: tbًā

HELP OVER THE PHONE

Gigi: Thank you for calling Sports Recreation Center. How may I help you?

Colette: I purchased an exercise bike from your store a couple months ago, and I am having problems with it. It stopped working and I need to have it repaired.

Gigi: Let me connect you to the Service department. One moment please.

Angela: Service department, this is Angela. How can I help you?

Colette: I bought an exercise bike from Sports Center last year and it needs to be repaired.

Angela: What seems to be the problem?

Colette: I am not what happened, but the computer screen is black and doesn't turn on anymore.

Angela: Did you try to press the Start button?

Colette: Yes, and nothing turns on.

Angela: What is your bike model?

Colette: It is a Skull Crusher 420Z+, it's the one with the really cool basket in the front.

Angela: I can send a technician out to take a look at your bike. It will cost $5,000.00 for labor. Also, if we have to replace any parts, that will be extra. Sound like a deal?

Colette: That is expensive. Isn't the repair cost covered by warranty?

Angela: When did you purchase your bike?

Colette: About 3 months ago.

Angela: I am sorry. The standard warranty only covers 1 month. Did you buy extra warranty coverage at the time of purchase?

Colette: No, I did not. Are there any other options besides paying $5,000.00 for repair labor?

Angela: No, I am afraid not.

Colette: Darn it.

34. هيّا نذهب إلى حفلة موسيقية – Let's Go To A Concert
(hyā nḏhb ỉlى ḥflۃ mwsyqyۃ)

كيث: دانيال، سيمون، سوف تقام حفلة موسيقية في الحديقة الليلة مع موسيقيين عظيمين. هل تريدان الذهاب؟
kyṯ: dānyāl، symwn، swf tqām ḥflۃ mwsyqyۃ fy ālḥdyqۃ āllylۃ mʿ mwsyqyyn ʿẓymyn. hl trydān ālḏhāb؟

دانيال: أنا لا أعمل الليلة. إذًا أستطيع الذهاب بالتأكيد.
dānyāl: ỉnā lā ỉʿml āllylۃ. ỉḏًā ỉstṭyʿ ālḏhāb bāltỉkyd.

سايمون: أنا أيضًا، لِنذهب إذًا!
sāymwn: ỉnā ỉyḍًā، lnḏhb ỉḏًā!

دانيال: هناك الكثير من السيارات في الخارج هذه الليلة ...
dānyāl: hnāk ālkṯyr mn ālsyārāt fy ālḫārǧ hḏh āllylۃ ...

سايمون: نعم، لماذا هناك زحمة كبيرة في حركة المرور؟
sāymwn: nʿm، lmāḏā hnāk zḥmۃ kbyrۃ fy ḥrkۃ ālmrwr؟

كيث: ربما يتجه الناس نحو المتنزه للحفلة. إنها فرقة مشهورة جدًا وتلعب موسيقى جيدة.
kyṯ: rbmā ytǧh ālnās nḥw ālmtnzh llḥflۃ. ỉnhā frqۃ mšhwrۃ ǧdًā wtlʿb mwsyqى ǧydۃ.

دانيال: نعم. على مدى السنوات الأربع الماضية، لم أضيع أي حفلة من حفلاتهم. في كل مرة تأتي الفرقة إلى المدينة، أشتري تذكرة.
dānyāl: nʿm. ʿlى mdى ālsnwāt ālỉrbʿ ālmāḍyۃ، lm ỉḍyʿ ỉy ḥflۃ mn ḥflāthm. fy kl mrۃ tỉty ālfrqۃ ỉlى ālmdynۃ، ỉštry tḏkrۃ.

سايمون: منذ متى بدأت الفرقة تلعب هنا محليًا؟
sāymwn: mnḏ mtى bdˈt ālfrqة tlʿb hnā mḥlyًā؟

دانيال: لقد بدأوا تقليديًا منذ ست سنوات، والآن يلعبون كل عام في الأسبوع الأول من شهر يونيو.
dānyāl: lqd bdˈwā tqlydyًā mnḏ st snwāt، wālˈn ylʿbwn kl ʿām fy ālˈsbwʿ ālˈwl mn šhr ywnyw.

كيث: سايمون، أنت حقا سوف تستمتع هذا المساء. سيكون هناك موسيقى رائعة، والكثير من المرح، وبالتأكيد الكثير من الصراخ.
kyṯ: sāymwn، ˈnt ḥqā swf tstmtʿ hḏā ālmsāʾ. sykwn hnāk mwsyqى rāئʿة، wālkṯyr mn ālmrḥ، wbāltˈkyd ālkṯyr mn ālṣrāẖ.

سايمون: لا أستطيع الانتظار، يبدو أن هناك الكثير من المرح.
sāymwn: lā ˈstṭyʿ ālāntẓār، ybdw ˈn hnāk ālkṯyr mn ālmrḥ.

دانيال: أنا أفضل موسيقى راب العصابات؛ ومع ذلك، يجب أن أقول إن موسيقى الريف يمكن أن تكون ممتعة للاستماع إليها. من المستغرب أن أستطيع الاستماع إليها طوال اليوم.
dānyāl: ˈnā ˈfḍl mwsyqى rāb ālʿṣābāt؛ wmʿ ḏlk، yǧb ˈn ˈqwl ˌn mwsyqى ālryf ymkn ˈn tkwn mmtʿة llāstmāʿ ˌlyhā. mn ālmstġrb ˈn ˈstṭyʿ ālāstmāʿ ˌlyhā ṭwāl ālywm.

كيث: سايمون، أي نوع من الموسيقى تحب؟
kyṯ: sāymwn، ˈy nwʿ mn ālmwsyqى tḥb؟

سايمون: أوه، أنا أحب جميع أنواع الموسيقى طالما أنها ليست عدوانية.
sāymwn: ˈwh، ˈnā ˈḥb ǧmyʿ ˈnwāʿ ālmwsyqى ṭālmā ˈnhā lyst ʿdwānyة.

دانيال: واو، الملعب ممتلئ بالناس! أنا مندهش من عدد الأشخاص الذين قدموا للحفل. من الجيد أننا هنا!
dānyāl: wāw، ālmlʿb mmtlئ bālnās! ˈnā mndhš mn ʿdd ālˈšẖāṣ ālḏyn qdmwā llḥfl. mn ālǧyd ˈnnā hnā!

LET'S GO TO A CONCERT

Keith: Hey Danielle, Simon, there is a concert in the park tonight with a great line up. Do you want to go?

Danielle: I don't work tonight so I can definitely go.

Simon: Me too, let's go!

Danielle: There's a ton of cars out tonight...

Simon: Yea, why is the traffic so heavy?

Keith: People are probably heading toward the park for the concert. It's a very popular band and they play really good music.

Danielle: Yes, they do. For the last four years, I have never missed one of their concerts. Every time I find out that the band is coming to town I buy a ticket right away.

Simon: How long ago did the band start playing here locally?

Danielle: They started a tradition six years ago and now every year they play the whole first week of June.

Keith: Simon, you are really going to enjoy this evening. There will be good great music, a lot of jumping around, and definitely a lot of shouting. They may even have a mosh pit.

Simon: I can't wait, it sounds like a lot fun.

Danielle: My favorite is gangster rap music; however, I have to say that country music can be pleasant to listen to. Surprisingly, I can listen to it all day long.

Keith: Simon, what kind of music do you like?

Simon: Oh, I like all kinds of music as long as it is not aggressive.

Danielle: Wow, the stadium is packed with people! I'm surprised at the number of people who have already shown up for the concert. It's a good thing we're here already!

35. القيام بخطط – Making Plans
(ālqyām bẖṭṭ)

كوني: ليزا، أخبريني عن خططك لعطلة نهاية الأسبوع القادمة؟
kwny: lyzā، ʾẖbryny ʿn ẖṭṭk lʿṭlẗ nhāyẗ ālʾsbwʿ ālqādmẗ؟

ليزا: لا أعرف. هل ترغبين في أن نتقابل ونقوم بشيء ما؟
lyzā: lā ʾʿrf. hl trġbyn fy ʾn ntqābl wnqwm bšyʾ mā؟

سارة: ما رأيكما بالذهاب لمشاهدة فيلم؟ فيAMC 24 على طريق باركر فهو يعرض *If You Leave Me, I Delete You.*
sār:ẗ mā rʾykmā bālḏhāb lmšāhdẗ fylm؟ fy AMC 24 ʿlى ṭryq bārkr fhw yʿrḍ If You Leave Me, I Delete You.

كوني: لقد كنت أرغب في مشاهدته! كأنكِ تقرأين أفكاري. هل تريدان الخروج لتناول العشاء قبل ذلك؟
kwny: lqd knt ʾrġb fy mšāhdth! kʾnk tqrʾyn ʾfkāry. hl trydān ālẖrwğ ltnāwl ālʿšāʾ qbl ḏlk؟

سارة: جيد جدًا. أين تريدان أن نلتقي؟
sār:ẗ ğyd ğdًā. ʾyn trydān ʾn nltqy؟

ليزا: لِنلتقي في Red Rooster House. لقد مرّ بعض الوقت منذ أن كنت هناك آخر مرة.
lyzā: lnltqy fy. Red Rooster House lqd mrّ bʿḍ ālwqt mnḏ ʾn knt hnāk ʾ̄ẖr mrẗ.

كوني: فكرة جيدة مرة أخرى. سمعت أنهم أصبحوا يقدمون معكرونة جديدة. بالتأكيد هي جيدة لأن Red Rooster House دائمًا تقدم أفضل الأطعمة الإيطالية في المدينة.

kwny: fkrẗ ǧydẗ mrẗ ʾḫrى. smʿt ʾnhm ʾṣbḥwā yqdmwn mʿkrwnẗ ǧdydẗ. bāltʾkyd hy ǧydẗ lʾn Red Rooster House dāʾٕmā̈ tqdm ʾfḍl ālʾṭʿmẗ ālʾٕyṭālyẗ fy ālmdynẗ.

سارة: متى نلتقي إذًا؟

sārẗ: mtى nltqy ʾٕḏā̈؟

ليزا: حسنًا، الفيلم يعرض الساعة 1:00 ظهرًا والساعة 2:00 ظهرًا والساعة 4:00 عصرًا والساعة 6:00 مساءً.

lyzā: ḥsnā̈، ālfylm yʿrḍ ālsāʿẗ 1:00 ẓhrā̈ wālsāʿẗ 2:00 ẓhrā̈ wālsāʿẗ 4:00 ʿṣrā̈ wālsāʿẗ 6:00 msāʾ̈.

كوني: لِماذا لا نذهب إلى عرض الساعة 4:00 مساءً؟ يمكننا أن نلتقي في Red Rooster House الساعة 1:00. هذا سيوفر لنا وقتًا كافيًا.

kwny: lmāḏā lā nḏhb ʾٕlى ʿrḍ ālsāʿẗ 4:00 msāʾ̈؟ ymknnā ʾn nltqy fy Red Rooster House ālsāʿẗ 1:00. hḏā sywfr lnā wqtā̈ kāfyā̈.

MAKING PLANS

Connie: Lisa, tell me... What are your plans for this upcoming weekend?

Lisa: I don't know. Do you want to get together and do something?

Sarah: How do you feel about going to see a movie? AMC 24 is showing *If You Leave Me, I Delete You.*

Connie: I've been wanting to see that! It's like you read my mind. Do you want to go out to dinner beforehand?

Sarah: That's fine with me. Where do you want to meet?

Lisa: Let's meet at the Red Rooster House. It's been a while since I've been there.

Connie: Good idea again. I heard they just came out with a new pasta. It should be good because Red Rooster House always has the best Italian food in town.

Sarah: When should we meet?

Lisa: Well, the movie is showing at 1:00PM, 2:00PM, 4:00PM and 6:00PM.

Connie: Why don't we go to the 4:00PM show? We can meet at Red Rooster House at 1PM. That will give us enough time.

36. العطلة الشتوية – WINTER BREAK

(ālʿṭlẗ ālštwyẗ)

ترينت: جاريد، إذا كنت على استعداد للذهاب فقط ارمِ جميع أغراضك في صندوق السيارة واركب في المقعد الأمامي.

trynt: ğāryd، !ḏā knt ʿlى āstʿdād llḏhāb fqṭ ārm ğmyʿ ˈiġrāḍk fy ṣndwq ālsyārẗ wārkb fy ālmqʿd ālˈimāmy.

جاريد: حسنًا، ترينت. شكرًا لتوصيلك لي للمنزل. في العادة، يصطحبني والداي، لكنهم اضطرا إلى العمل إلى وقت متأخر الليلة.

ğāryd: ḥsnā، trynt. škrā ltwṣylk ly llmnzl. fy ālʿādẗ، yṣṭḥbny wāldāy، lknhm āḍṭrā !lى ālʿml !lى wqt mtˈiẖr āllylẗ.

ترينت: لا تقلق، يسعدني أن أقدم يد المساعدة.

trynt: lā tqlq، ysʿdny ˈin ˈiqdm yd ālmsāʿdẗ.

جاريد: بالمناسبة، متى تكون لعبتنا القادمة لكرة السلة؟

ğāryd: bālmnāsbẗ، mtى tkwn lʿbtnā ālqādmẗ lkrẗ ālsl؟ẗ

ترينت: إنها في وقت ما بعد العطلة الشتوية، لكن على أي حال، لا هناك يزال وقت طويل من الآن. هل وضعت أي خطط للعطلة؟

trynt: !nhā fy wqt mā bʿd ālʿṭlẗ ālštwyẗ، lkn ʿlˈi ى y ḥāl، lā hnāk yzāl wqt ṭwyl mn ālˈin. hl wḍʿt ˈiy ẖṭṭ llʿṭl؟ẗ

جاريد: لا, فقط قررت الذهاب لممارسة كرة السلة، وسأعمل فقط.

ğāryd: lā، fqṭ qrrt ālḏhāb lmmārsẗ krẗ ālslẗ، wsˈiʿml fqṭ.

ترينت: تعمل؟ هل حصلت على وظيفة جديدة أم أنك لا تزال تعمل في Twisters؟

trynt: tʿml؟ hl ḥṣlt ʿlى wẓyfẗ ğdydˈi ẗm ˈink lā tzāl tʿml fy Twisters؟

جاريد: حسنًا، كانت Twisters أول وظيفة جيدة وكان زملائي رائعين حقًا في العمل معهم. ومع ذلك، كان جدول العمل صعبًا للغاية مما جعل من الصعب عليّ الذهاب إلى المدرسة والعمل.

ğāryd: ḥsnā، kānt Twisters ˈwl wẓyfẗ ğydẗ wkān zmlāئy rāئʿyn ḥqā fy ālʿml mʿhm. wmʿ ḏlk، kān ğdwl ālʿml ṣʿbā llġāyẗ mmā ğʿl mn ālṣʿb ʿlyّ ālḏhāb إlى ālmdrsẗ wālʿml.

ترينت: حسنًا، ماذا تفعل الآن في وظيفتك الجديدة؟

trynt: ḥsnā، māḏā tfʿl ālˈn fy wẓyftk ālğdydẗ؟

جاريد: أنا أعمل في مجال مبيعات التكنولوجيا. إنها في مركز الاتصال. كان الأمر صعبًا بعض الشيء في البداية، لكنني الآن معتاد على التحدث إلى الغرباء على الهاتف.

ğāryd: ˈnā ˈʿml fy mğāl mbyʿāt āltknwlwğyā. إnhā fy mrkz ālātṣāl. kān ālˈmr ṣʿbā bʿḍ ālšyʾ fy ālbdāyẗ، lknny ālˈn mʿtād ʿlى āltḥdṯ إlى ālġrbāʾ ʿlى ālhātf.

ترينت: أوه، هذا يبدو رائعًا. متى بدأت عملك الجديد؟

trynt: ˈwh، hḏā ybdw rāئʿā. mtى bdˈt ʿmlk ālğdyd؟

جاريد: لقد بدأت مع TechAmerica منذ 1 أكتوبر. هل لديك أي خطط للعطلة؟

ğāryd: lqd bdˈt mʿ TechAmerica mnḏ 1 ˈktwbr. hl ldyk ˈy ḫṭṭ llʿṭlẗ؟

ترينت: أخطط لرحلة الى الجليد في آسبن. يجب أن تأتي إذا لم تكن مشغولًا في العمل الجديد.

trynt: ˈḫṭṭ lrḥlẗ ālى ālğlyd fy ˈsbn. yğb ˈn tˈty إḏā lm tkn mšġwlā fy ālʿml ālğdyd.

جاريد: أوه، هذا يبدو ممتعًا! شكرًا لدعوتك.

ğāryd: ˈwh، hḏā ybdw mmtʿā! škrā ldʿwtk.

WINTER BREAK

Trent: Hey Jared, if you're ready to go just throw your all of your stuff in the trunk and ride in the front seat.

Jared: Alright, Trent. Thank you for giving me a ride home. Usually my parents pick me up, but they had to work late tonight.

Trent: No worries, I'm glad I could help.

Jared: By the way, when is our next basketball game?

Trent: It is sometime after winter break, but anyways it's a long time from now. Have you made any plans for the break though?

Jared: Not really. Other than going to basketball practice, I'll just be working.

Trent: Working? Did you get a new job or are you still working at Twisters?

Jared: Well, Twisters was a good first job and the people were really great to work with. However, the schedule was very demanding which made it difficult to go to school and work.

Trent: Well, what are you doing now at your new job?

Jared: I am working in technology sales. It's at a call center. It was a little difficult at first, but now I am used to talking to strangers on the phone.

Trent: Oh, that sounds great. When did you start the new job?

Jared: I have been with TechAmerica since October 1st. Do you have any plans for break?

Trent: I am planning a snowboarding trip to Aspen. You should come if you're not too busy at the new job.

Jared: Oh, that sounds like fun! Thank you for the invitation.

37. زيارة الطبيب – VISITING THE DOCTOR
(zyārẗ ālṭbyb)

الطبيب: صباح الخير آمي.

ālṭbyb: ṣbāḥ ālḫyr ꞌmy.

آمي: صباح الخير دكتور.

ꞌmy: ṣbāḥ ālḫyr dktwr.

الطبيب: عند الاطلاع على معلوماتك، أرى أنكِ بدأتِ تشعرين بالتعب منذ حوالي شهر، ثم بدأتِ تعانين من الصداع النصفي.

ālṭbyb: ʿnd ālāṭlāʿ ʿlى mʿlwmātk، ꞌrꞌ ꞌnk bdꞌt tšʿryn āltʿb mnḏ ḥwāly šhr، ṯm bdꞌt tʿānyn mn ālṣdāʿ ālnṣfy.

لديكِ أيضًا اضطراب في المعدة وحمّى؟

ldyk ꞌyḍā ādṭrāb fy ālmʿdẗ wḥmى؟

آمي: لا يا دكتور.

ꞌmy: lā yā dktwr.

الطبيب: سأجري فحصًا جسديًا سريعًا.

ālṭbyb: sꞌǧry fḥṣā ǧsdyā sryʿā.

الطبيب: أرجوكِ خذي نفسًا عميقًا، احبسي أنفاسك، ثم أخرجي النفس. مرة أخرى من فضلك.

ālṭbyb: ꞌrǧwk ḫḏy nfsā ʿmyqā، āḥbsy ꞌnfāsk، ṯm ꞌḫrǧy ālnfs. mrꞌẗ ꞌḫrى mn fḍlk.

الطبيب: هل قمتِ بإجراء أي تغييرات على نظامك الغذائي لأن هناك تدهورًا في وزنك مؤخرًا؟

āltṭbyb: hl qmtِ bإğrāʾ ʾy tġyyrāt ʿlى nẓāmk ālġḏāئy lʾn hnāk tdhwrًā fy wznk mؤḫrًā؟

آمي: خسرت خمسة أرطال مؤخرًا، لكنني لم أغيّر حميتي على الإطلاق.

ʾmy: ḫsrt ḫmsة ʾrṭāl mؤḫrًā، lknny lm ʾġyّr ḥmyty ʿlى ālإṭlāq.

الطبيب: هل تعانين من الأرق صدفة؟

āltṭbyb: hl tʿānyn mn ālʾrq ṣdfة؟

آمي: من الصعب عليّ النوم عندما أريد الخلود للنوم. فأنا أستيقظ كثيرًا خلال الليل.

ʾmy: mn ālṣʿb ʿlyّ ālnwm ʿndmā ʾryd ālḫlwd llnwm. fʾnā ʾstyqẓ kṯyrًā ḫlāl āllyl.

الطبيب: هل تشربين الكحول أو تدخنين السجائر؟

āltṭbyb: hl tšrbyn ālkḥwl ʾw tdḫnyn ālsğāئr؟

آمي: لا.

ʾmy: lā.

الطبيب: يبدو أن لديكِ التهاب رئوي. بالإضافة إلى ذلك، لا أرى أية مشاكل أخرى. الآن، احصلي على بعض الراحة وقومي ببعض التمارين الرياضية. سأعطيكي وصفة للالتهاب الرئوي. هل لديكِ حساسية من أي أدوية؟

āltṭbyb: ybdw ʾn ldykِ ālthāb rئwy. bālإḍāfة إlى ḏlk، lā ʾrى ʾyة mšākl ʾḫrى. ālʾn، āḥṣly ʿlى bʿḍ ālrāḥة wqwmy bbʿḍ āltmāryn ālryāḍyة. sʾʿṭyky wṣfة llālthāb ālrئwy. hl ldykِ ḥsāsyة mn ʾy ʾdwyة؟

آمي: لا أدري.

ʾmy: lā ʾdry.

الطبيب: حسنًا. خذي هذا الدواء ثلاث مرات في اليوم بعد تناول الطعام.
ālṭbyb: ḥsnā̋. ẖḏy hḏā āldwā' ṯlāṯ mrāt fy ālywm bʿd tnāwl ālṭʿām.

آمي: شكرًا لك يا دكتور.

ǐmy: škrā̋ lk yā dktwr.

الطبيب: أنت دائمًا مرحّب بك.

ālṭbyb: ỉnt dāئmā̋ mrḥb bk.

VISITING THE DOCTOR

Doctor: Good morning, Amy.

Amy: Good morning, Doctor.

Doctor: Looking at your information, I see that you started feeling tired about a month ago, and then you started having migraines.

You have also had an upset stomach and fever?

Amy: No, doctor.

Doctor: Let me do a quick physical checkup.

Doctor: Please take a deep breath, hold your breath, and then exhale. One more time please.

Doctor: Have you made any changes to your diet or seen fluctuation in your weight recently?

Amy: I lost five pounds recently, but I haven't changed my diet at all.

Doctor: By chance do you suffer from insomnia?

Amy: It is difficult for me to fall asleep when I go to bed. I also wake up a lot during the night.

Doctor: Do you drink or smoke cigarettes?

Amy: No.

Doctor: It appears that you have pneumonia. Besides that, I do not see any other problems. For now, get some rest and do some exercise.

I am going to give you a prescription for the pneumonia. Are you allergic to any medications?

Amy: Not that I am aware of.

Doctor: Alright. Take this medication three times a day after you eat.

Amy: Thank you, Doctor.

Doctor: You are welcome.

38. السوق – The Market
(ālswq)

لورا: جوي، قبل أن تغادر أمي للعمل هذا الصباح طلبت مني أن أذهب لشراء البقالة. المشكلة هي أنني بحاجة لإنهاء مشروع مدرستي. هل يمكنك الذهاب عوضًا عني؟
lwrā: ğwy، qbl ỉn tġādr ỉmy ll‘ml hḏā ālṣbāḥ ṭlbt mny ỉn ỉḏhb lšrā’ ālbqāl.ẗ ālmšklẗ hy ỉnny bḥāğẗ lỉnhā’ mšrw‘ mdrsty. hl ymknk ālḏhāb ‘wḍā ‘ny؟

جوي: لقد أنهيت واجباتي، لذا يمكنني الذهاب إلى المتجر نيابة عنك. ماذا تريد منك أمي أن تشتري؟
ğwy: lqd ỉnhyt wāğbāty، lḏā ymknny ālḏhāb ỉlى ālmtğr nyābẗ ‘nk. māḏā tryd mnk ỉmy ỉn tštry؟

لورا: بالإضافة إلى الدجاج والأسماك والخضروات، يمكننا شراء أي شيء آخر نريده للوجبات الخفيفة ووجبة الإفطار. لقد أرادتني أن أشتري ما يكفينا من البقالة طوال الأسبوع.
lwrā: bālỉḍāfẗ ỉlى āldğāğ wālỉsmāk wālḫḍrwāt، ymknnā šrā’ ỉy šy’ ỉḫr nrydh llwğbāt ālḫfyfẗ wwğbẗ ālỉfṭār. lqd ỉrādtny ỉn ỉštry mā ykfynā mn ālbqālẗ ṭwāl ālỉsbw‘.

جوي: هل هناك أي شيء معين تريدينه للإفطار؟
ğwy: hl hnāk ỉy šy’ m‘yn trydynh llỉfṭār؟

لورا: بعض دقيق الشوفان كالمعتاد.
lwrā: b‘ḍ dqyq ālšwfān kālm‘tād.

جوي: أنا لا أرغب في دقيق الشوفان كل يوم. سأشتري بعض الفطائر والشراب بعد ذلك.
ğwy: ỉnā lā ỉrġb fy dqyq ālšwfān kl ywm. sỉštry bʿḍ ālfṭāỷr wālšrāb bʿd ḏlk.

لورا: إذا كنت تستطيع العثور عليها، يمكنك الحصول على الفطائر الخالية من الغلوتين في قسم الأكلات الصحية من فضلك. أريد أن أرى ما إذا كان طعمها مختلفًا.
lwrā: ḻḏā knt tstṭyʿ ālʿṯwr ʿlyhā، ymknk ālḥṣwl ʿlى ālfṭāỷr ālẖālyẗ mn ālġlwtyn fy qsm ālỉklāt ālṣḥyẗ mn fḍlk. ỉryd ỉn ỉrى mā ḻḏā kān ṭʿmhā mẖtlfā̹.

جوي: هل ما زال هناك ما يكفي من القهوة والكريمة لأمي وأبي؟
ğwy: hl mā zāl hnāk mā ykfy mn ālqhwẗ wālkrymẗ lỉmy wỉby؟

لورا: نعم مازال. في الواقع، يجب عليك شراء بعض الحليب أيضًا. فقد شارف على الانتهاء.
lwrā: nʿm māzāl. fy ālwāqʿ، yğb ʿlyk šrāʾ bʿḍ ālḥlyb ỉyḍā̹. fqd šārf ʿlى ālānthāʾ.

جوي: وكذلك ماذا تريدين للوجبات الخفيفة؟
ğwy: wkḏlk māḏā trydyn llwğbāt ālẖfyf؟ẗ

لورا: بعض الرقائق ستكون كافية. ربما تريد بعض الكوكيز بالشوكولاتة.
lwrā: bʿḍ ālrqāỷq stkwn kāfy.ẗ rbmā tryd bʿḍ ālkwkyz bālšwkwlātẗ.

جوي: أنا أعرف نفسي لذا من المحبذ أن أكتب كل هذه الأشياء وإلا سأنساها عندما أصل إلى السوق. أنا أكره أن أضطر إلى القيام بمشيتين!
ğwy: ỉnā ỉʿrf nfsy lḏā mn ālmḥbḏ ỉn ỉktb kl hḏh ālỉšyāʾ wḻlā sỉnsāhā ʿndmā ỉṣl ḻlى ālswq. ỉnā ỉkrh ỉn ỉḍṭr ḻlى ālqyām bmšytyn!

The Market

Laura: Joy, before mom left for work this morning, she asked me to go grocery shopping. The problem is that I need to finish my school project. Can you go for me?

Joy: I am finished with my chores, so I can go to the store for you. What did mom want you to buy?

Laura: Besides chicken, fish and vegetables, we can buy whatever else we want for snacks and breakfast. She basically wanted me to buy enough groceries for the entire week.

Joy: Is there anything specifically you want for breakfast?

Laura: I guess some oatmeal as usual.

Joy: I don't want oatmeal every day. I will buy some pancakes and syrup then.

Laura: If you can find it, get the new gluten free pancakes in the health section please. I want to see if it tastes any different.

Joy: Is there still enough coffee and cream for mom and dad?

Laura: Yes, we do. In fact, you should buy some milk also. We almost out of it.

Joy: Next, what do you want for snacks?

Laura: Some chips would be fine with me. You probably want your chocolate cookies.

Joy: Knowing myself it's probably better that I write all these things down or else I will forget them by the time I get to the market. I would hate to have to make two trips!

39. دعنا نحصل على شقة – LET'S GET AN APARTMENT
(dʿnā nḥṣl ʿlى šqة)

باتريك: جوش. ما الذي تفعله هنا؟

bātryk: ğwš. mā āldy tfʿlh hnā؟

جوش: أنا أبحث عن شقة للإيجار. ما الذي تفعله أنت هنا؟ هل تبحث عن شقة أيضًا؟

ğwš: ʾnā ʾbḥṯ ʿn šqة llʾyğār. mā āldy tfʿlh ʾnt hnā؟ hl tbḥṯ ʿn šqʾ ةyḍā؟

باتريك: نعم. منزل والدي بعيد، لذا أرغب في ايجاد شقة أقرب إلى المدرسة وعملي.

bātryk: nʿm. mnzl wāldy bʿyd، ldā ʾrġb fy āyğād šqʾ ةqrb ʾlى ālmdrsة wʿmly.

جوش: حسنًا، هذا ما أفكر به. لم أقرر بعد ما إذا كنت أرغب في الإقامة في مساكن الطلبة أو الحصول على شقتي الخاصة.

ğwš: ḥsnā، hdā mā ʾfkr bh. lm ʾqrr bʿd mā ʾdā knt ʾrġb fy ālʾqāmة fy msākn ālṭlbʾ ةw ālḥṣwl ʿlى šqty ālḫāṣة.

باتريك: إذًا، ما الذي تبحث عنه؟

bātryk: ʾdā، mā āldy tbḥṯ ʿnh؟

جوش: سوف أكون صريح. كل ما أحتاجه هو مكان كبير بما فيه الكفاية لسريري ومكتبي بالطبع. يجب أن يكون هناك مطبخ حتى أتمكن من طهي وجباتي وتوفير القليل من المال.

ğwš: swf ʾkwn ṣryḥ. kl mā ʾḥtāğh hw mkān kbyr bmā fyh ālkfāyة lsryry wmktby bālṭbʿ. yğb ʾn ykwn hnāk mṭbḫ ḥtʾ ىtmkn mn ṭhy wğbāty wtwfyr ālqlyl mn ālmāl.

باتريك: يبدو هذا مثل ما أبحث عنه أيضًا. لا أستطيع العمل بدوام كامل كما فعلت خلال فصل الصيف. سأقضي معظم وقتي في الدراسة لذا لن أتمكن من العمل بنفس القدر. كل ما أحتاجه هو شقة آمنة وهادئة ونظيفة.

bātryk: ybdw hḏā mṯl mā ỉbḥṯ ʿnh ỉyḍًā. lā ỉstṭyʿ ālʿml bdwām kāml kmā fʿlt ḫlāl fṣl ālṣyf. sỉqḍy mʿẓm wqty fy āldrāsẗ lḏā ln ỉtmkn mn ālʿml bnfs ālqdr. kl mā ỉḥtāğh hw šqẗ ảmnẗ whādỷẗ wnẓyfẗ.

جوش: الأمر الآخر يتعلق بدفع ثمن شقة كاملة بنفسي. معظم الأماكن التي رأيتها باهظة للغاية.

ğwš: ālỉmr ālảḫr ytʿlq bdfʿ ṯmn šqẗ kāmlẗ bnfsy. mʿẓm ālỉmākn ālty rỉythā bāhẓẗ llġāyẗ.

باتريك: هل فكرت في مشاركة شقة؟ إذا كنت تريد، يمكننا العثور على شقة من غرفتي نوم ومشاركتها. قد يكون أرخص بهذه الطريقة.

bātryk: hl fkrt fy mšārkẗ šqẗ؟ ỉḏā knt tryd، ymknnā ālʿṯwr ʿlى šqẗ mn ġrfty nwm wmšārkthā. qd ykwn ỉrḫṣ bhḏh ālṭryqẗ.

جوش: يمكن لهذا أن يحل مشكلتنا. هل تريد أن نجرب ذلك؟

ğwš: ymkn lhḏā ỉn yḥl mškltnā. hl tryd ỉn nğrb ḏlk؟

باتريك: نعم، هذه فكرة رائعة. دعنا نذهب إلى التحقق من هذا ونرى ما إذا كان سعجبنا.

bātryk: nʿm، hḏh fkrẗ rāỷʿẗ. dʿnā nḏhb ỉlى ālthqq mn hḏā wnrى mā ỉḏā kān sʿğbnā.

LET'S GET AN APARTMENT

Patrick: Hey, Josh. What are you doing here?

Josh: I am looking for an apartment to rent. What are you doing here? Are you looking for an apartment also?

Patrick: Yes. My parents' house is really far away so I'd like to find an apartment that is closer to school and my job.

Josh: Ok, that makes sense. I still haven't decided if I want to stay in the dorms or get my own apartment.

Patrick: So, what are you looking for?

Josh: I don't need much to be honest. All I need is a place big enough for my bed and desk. Of course, it needs to have a kitchen so that I can cook my meals and save a little bit of money.

Patrick: That sounds like what I'm looking for too. I can't work full-time like I did during the summer. I will be spending most of my time studying so I won't be able to work as much. All I need is something safe, quiet and clean.

Josh: The other issue is paying for an entire apartment for myself. Most places I have seen are very expensive.

Patrick: Have you thought about sharing an apartment? If you want, we can find a two-bedroom apartment and share it. It may be cheaper that way.

Josh: That could solve our problem.

Josh: Do you want to try it?

Patrick: Yes, that could be a great idea. Let's go check this one out and see if we like it.

40. موقف الامتياز – The Concesssion Stand
(mwqf ālāmtyāz)

سايمون: هناك موقف لبيع الطعام هناك. هل تريدان شيئًا؟
sāymwn: hnāk mwqf lbyʿ ālṭʿām hnāk. hl trydān šyئā؟

دانييل: لا شيء بالنسبة لي، شكرًا. عندي زجاجة مياه.
dānyyl: lā šyʾ bālnsbة ly، škrā. ʿndy zǧāǧة myāh.

كيث: أريد كيس شيبس وبيرة باردة. هل أنت متأكد أنك لا تريد هوت دوغ يا دانييل؟
kyṯ: ịryd kys šybs w byrة bārd.ة hl ịnt mtịkd ịnk lā tryd hwt dwġ yā dānyyl؟

دانييل: نعم متأكد تمامًا. أمي تطبخ عشاء لذيذ من شرائح اللحم، ولا أريد أن أتناول الكثير من الطعام هنا.
dānyyl: nʿm mtịkd tmāmā. ịmy tṭbẖ ʿšāʾ ldyḏ mn šrāئḥ āllḥm، wlā ịryd ịn ịtnāwl ālkṯyr mn ālṭʿām hnā.

كيث: دانييل، أنت محظوظ جدًا أن يكون لديك طباخ جيد مثل امك. سايمون، عليك أن تذوق فطائر التوت خاصتها في أحد هذه الأيام. بصراحة، ليس هناك فطيرة أفضل منها في هذه البلدة بأكملها.
kyṯ: dānyyl، ịnt mḥẓwẓ ǧdā ịn ykwn ldyk ṭbāẖ ǧyd mṯl āmk. sāymwn، ʿlyk ịn tḏwq fṭāئr āltwt ẖāṣthā fy ịḥd hḏh ālịyām. bṣrāḥ،ة lys hnāk fṭyrị ةfḍl mnhā fy hḏh ālbldة bịkmlhā.

دانييل: فى الحقيقة، أمي تخبز فطيرة توت الليلة! سأترك لك قطعة يا سايمون.
dānyyl: fى ālḥqyqị ،ةmy tẖbz fṭyrة twt āllyl!ة sịtrk lk qṭʿة yā sāymwn.

سايمون: لا تستفزني في الوقت المناسب! أنا أحب ذلك.
sāymwn: lā tstfzny fy ālwqt ālmnāsb! ʾnā ʾḥb ḏlk.

دانييل: ماذا عنكِ يا كيث؟ قطعة من الكعكة بالنسبة لك أيضًا؟
dānyyl: māḏā ʿnk yā kyṯ؟ qṭʿẗ mn ālkʿkẗ bālnsbẗ lk ʾyḍā؟

سايمون: كيث، من الأفضل أن تحصلي على وجبتك الخفيفة والبيرة الآن إذا كنتِ لا تزالين تريدين ذلك. الساعة 3:00 مساءً تقريبًا، والعرض على وشك أن يبدأ.
sāymwn: kyṯ، mn ālʾfḍl ʾn tḥṣly ʿlى wǧbtk ālḫfyfẗ wālbyrẗ ālʾn ʾḏā knt lā tzālyn trydyn ḏlk. ālsāʿ3:00 ẗ msāʾً tqrybā، wālʿrḍ ʿlى wšk ʾn ybdʾ.

كيث: آخر فرصة لك للحصول على شيء ما. هل أنت متأكد من أنك لا تريد أي شيء؟
kyṯ: ʾḫr frṣẗ lk llḥṣwl ʿlى šyʾ mā. hl ʾnt mtʾkd mn ʾnk lā tryd ʾy šyʾ؟

دانييل: أنا متأكد، شكرًا لك كيث.
dānyyl: ʾnā mtʾkd، škrā lk kyṯ.

سايمون: أنا ايضًا كيث.
sāymwn: ʾnā āyḍā kyṯ.

كيث: حسنًا، احجزا مقعدي وسوف أعود مباشرة.
kyṯ: ḥsnā، āḥǧzā mqʿdy wswf ʾʿwd mbāšrẗ.

The Concession Stand

Simon: There is a food stand over there. Do you two want anything?

Danielle: Nothing for me, thanks. I already have my bottle of water.

Keith: I want a bag of chips and a cold beer. Are you sure you do not want a hot dog, Danielle?

Danielle: I am quite sure. My mom is cooking a good steak dinner, and I want to make sure I don't eat too much here.

Keith: Danielle, you are so lucky to have such a good cook for a mother. Simon, you have to taste her blueberry pie one of these days. Honestly, there's no better pie in this whole town.

Danielle: In fact, my mom is baking her blueberry pie tonight! I you would like, I will save you a piece, Simon.

Simon: Don't tease me with a good time! I would love that.

Danielle: How about you, Keith? A piece of cake for you too?

Simon: Keith, you better get your snacks and beer now if you still want them. It is almost 3:00PM, and the show is about to start.

Keith: Last chance to get something. Are you guys sure you don't want anything?

Danielle: I am sure, thank you Keith.

Simon: Me neither, Keith.

Keith: Ok, save my seat and I will be right back.

41. وقت الغداء – LUNCHTIME
(wqt ālġdā')

إميلي: تريشيا، هل يمكنني استعارة هاتفك للاتصال بأمي بعد الغداء؟
!myly: tryšyā، hl ymknny āst'ārة hātfk llātṣāl bꞌmy b'd ālġdā'؟

تريشيا: نعم، بالطبع يا إميلي. سلمي عليها.
tryšyā: n'm، bālṭb' yā !myly. slmy 'lyhā.

ميرا: إميلي، هل يمكنك تمرير الفلفل لي من فضلك؟
myrā: !myly، hl ymknk tmryr ālflfl ly mn fḍlk؟

إميلي: بالتأكيد، تفضلي.
!myly: bāltꞌkyd، tfḍly.

ميرا: والملح أيضًا من فضلك. شكرًا لك.
myrā: wālmlḥ ꞌyḍā mn fḍlk. škrā lk.

إميلي: لا شكر على واجب.
!myly: lā škr 'lى wāğb.

تريشيا: هل تمانعان إذا توقفنا عند مكتبة طريق ستراند في طريقنا إلى الفيلم؟
tryšyā: hl tmān'ān !ḏā twqfnā 'nd mktbة ṭryq strānd fy ṭryqnā !lى ālfylm؟

إميلي: لا، على الإطلاق.
!myly: lā، lى āl!ṭlāq.

ميرا: سمعت أن لديهم سلسلة كتب جديدة لذلك أحب أن أتوقف وأتحقق من ذلك.
myrā: sm't ꞌn ldyhm slslة ktb ğdydة lḏlk ꞌḥb ꞌn ꞌtwqf wꞌtḥqq mn ḏlk.

تريشيا: طلبت الكثير من الطعام. هل يريد أي شخص بتجربة بعض من طعامي؟
tryšyā: ṭlbt ālkṯyr mn ālṭʿām. hl yryd ̉y šẖṣ btğrbẗ bʿḍ mn ṭʿāmy؟

إميلي: نعم، أود لانه يبدو لذيذ.
̹myly: nʿm، ̉wd lānh ybdw lḏyḏ.

تريشيا: ماذا عنك يا ميرا؟
tryšyā: māḏā ʿnk yā myrā؟

ميرا: لا، شكراً لك. لدي ما يكفي من الطعام بالفعل.
myrā: lā ، škrāً lk. ldy mā ykfy mn ālṭʿām bālfʿl.

إميلي: تريشيا، هل ترغبين في تذوق واحدة من فاجيتس بلدي؟
̹myly: tryšyā، hl trġbyn fy tḏwq wāḥdẗ mn fāğyts bldy؟

تريشيا: نعم، من فضلك.
tryšyā: nʿm ، mn fḍlk.

إميلي: تفضلي هل تريدين أخرى؟
̹myly: tfḍly hl trydyn ̉ẖr؟ى

تريشيا: أوه، هذا أكثر من كافي! شكرا لك.
tryšyā: ̉wh ، hḏā ̉kṯr mn kāfy! škrā lk.

ميرا: اعتقد أننا انتهينا من الأكل؟ يجب أن نرحل الآن لتجنب زحمة المرور؛ وإلا فسوف نتأخر.
myrā: āʿtqd ̉nnā ānthynā mn āl̉kl؟ yğb ̉n nrḥl āl̉n ltğnb zḥmẗ ālmrwr ؛ w̹lā fswf nt̉ẖr.

تريشيا: أنا على استعداد لمغادرة وقت ما تريدون.
tryšyā: ̉nā ʿlى āstʿdād lmġādrẗ wqt mā trydwn.

إميلي: إذن دعنا نذهب.
̹myly: ̹ḏn dʿnā nḏhb.

LUNCHTIME

Emily: Tricia, May I borrow your cell phone to call my mother after lunch?

Tricia: Yes, of course, Emily. Don't forget to tell her we said hello.

Maira: Emily, could you pass the pepper, please?

Emily: Certainly, here you are.

Maira: And the salt too, please. Thank you.

Emily: You're welcome.

Tricia: Would either of you mind if we stop by Strand Bookstore on the way to the movie?

Emily: No, not at all.

Maira: I heard they have a new book selection so I would love to stop by and check it out.

Tricia: I ordered too much food. Would anybody care to try some of my food?

Emily: Yes, I would like some. It looks delicious.

Tricia: How about you, Maira?

Maira: No, thank you. I have enough food already.

Emily: Tricia, would you like to taste one of my fajitas?

Tricia: Yes, please.

Emily: Here you go. Do you want another?

Tricia: Oh, that is more than enough! Thank you.

Maira: I imagine we are all finished eating? We should leave now to avoid the traffic; otherwise we will be late.

Tricia: I am ready to leave whenever you all are.

Emily: So am I. Let's go.

42. البحث عن وظيفة – SEARCHING FOR A JOB
(ālbḥṯ ʿn wẓyfẗ)

ماتيلدا: مرحبًا باولو، من الجيد أن أراك.
mātyldā: mrḥbā̃ bāwlw، mn ālğyd ʾn ʾrāk.

باولو: أنا أيضًا ماتيلدا. لقد مرّ وقت طويل منذ آخر مرة رأيتك فيها
bāwlw: ʾnā ʾyḍā̃ mātyldā. lqd mr̃ wqt ṭwyl mnḏ ʾ̄ḫr mrẗ rʾytk fyhā

ماتيلدا: نعم، آخر مرة رأينا بعضنا البعض كانت في عيد القديسين. كيف تجري الأمور معك؟
mātyldā: nʿm، ʾ̄ḫr mrẗ rʾynā bʿḍnā ālbʿḍ kānt fy ʿyd ālqdysyn. kyf tğry ālʾmwr mʿk؟

باولو: أنا بخير. سيكون من الأفضل لو عثرت على وظيفة جديدة.
bāwlw: ʾnā bḫyr. sykwn mn ālʾfḍl lw ʿṯrt ʿlى wẓyfẗ ğdydẗ.

ماتيلدا: لماذا تبحث عن وظيفة جديدة؟
mātyldā: lmāḏā tbḥṯ ʿn wẓyfẗ ğdyd؟ẗ

باولو: حسنًا، لقد تخرجت الأسبوع الماضي. الآن، أريد الحصول على وظيفة في مجال التمويل.
bāwlw: ḥsnā̃، lqd tḫrğt ālʾsbwʿ ālmāḍy. ālʾ̄n، ʾryd ālḥṣwl ʿlى wẓyfẗ fy mğāl āltmwyl.

ماتيلدا: هل بحثت كثيرًا عن وظيفة جديدة؟
mātyldā: hl bḥṯt kṯyrā̃ ʿn wẓyfẗ ğdyd؟ẗ

باولو: لا, لقد بدأت هذا الأسبوع.
bāwlw: lā, lqd bdʾt hḏā ālʾsbwʿ

ماتيلدا: هل أعددت السيرة الذاتية؟

mātyldā: hl ỉʿddt ālsyrẗ āldātyẗ?

باولو: أكيد.

bāwlw: ỉkyd.

ماتيلدا: لا داعي للقلق إذًا. إن لديك الكثير من الطموح وأعرف أنك ستضع كل طاقتك في الحصول على ما تريده. علاوة على ذلك، فإن سوق العمل ممتاز الآن، وجميع الشركات تحتاج إلى محللين ماليين.

mātyldā: lā dāʿy llqlq ỉḏā̃. ỉn ldyk ālkṯyr mn ālṭmwḥ wỉʿrf ỉnk stḍʿ kl ṭāqtk fy ālḥṣwl ʿlى mā trydh. ʿlāwẗ ʿlى ḏlk، fỉn swq ālʿml mmtāz ālȳn، wǧmyʿ ālšrkāt tḥtāǧ ỉlى mḥllyn mālyyn.

باولو: آمل ذلك. شكرًا على النصيحة.

bāwlw: ȳml ḏlk. škrā̃ ʿlى ālnṣyḥẗ.

Searching For A Job

Matilda: Hi Paolo, it is good to see you.

Paolo: Same here, Matilda. It has been a long time since I last saw you.

Matilda: Yes, the last time we saw each other was around Halloween. How is everything?

Paolo: I am doing OK. It would be better if I had a new job.

Matilda: Why are looking for a new job?

Paolo: Well, I graduated last week. Now, I want to get a job in the Finance field.

Matilda: Have you been looking for a new job for a while?

Paolo: I just started this week.

Matilda: You have prepared a resume, right?

Paolo: Yes.

Matilda: I wouldn't worry then. You have a lot of ambition and I know you will put all of your energy into getting what you want. Besides, the job market is really good right now, and all companies need financial analysts.

Paolo: I hope so. Thank you for the advice.

43. مقابلة الوظيفة – Job Interview
(mqāblẗ ālwẓyfẗ)

هيو: مرحبًا زاك. لنبدأ المقابلة. هل أنت جاهز؟
hyw: mrḥbā̈ zāk. lnbdʾ ālmqābl.ẗ hl ʾnt ğāhz؟

زاك: نعم، أنا كذلك.
zāk: nʿm، ʾnā kḏlk.

هيو: عظيم. أولاً، دعني أعرف بنفسي بشكل صحيح. أنا مدير الشركة اللوجستية. أحتاج إلى ملء منصب مستوى الدخول في أقرب وقت ممكن.
hyw: ʿẓym. ʾwlā̈، dʿny ʾʿrf bnfsy bškl ṣḥyḥ. ʾnā mdyr ālšrkẗ āllwğstyʾ .ẗḥtāğ ʾlى mlʾ mnṣb mstwى āldẖwl fy ʾqrb wqt mmkn.

زاك: هذا رائع. هل يمكن أن تحدثني قليلاً عن المنصب وما هي توقعاتك؟
zāk:hḏā rāئʿ. hl ymkn ʾn tḥdṯny qlylā̈ʿn ālmnṣb wmā hy twqʿātk؟

هيو: سيتعين على الموظف الجديد العمل عن كثب مع قسم التصنيع. هناك أيضًا شرط للتعامل مع البنك على أساس يومي.
hyw: sytʿyn ʿlى ālmwẓf ālğdyd ālʿml ʿn kṯb mʿ qsm āltṣnyʿ. hnāk ʾyḍā̈ šrṭ lltʿāml mʿ ālbnk ʿlʾ ىsās ywmy.

زاك: ما هي المؤهلات التي تحتاجها؟
zāk: mā hy ālmؤhlāt ālty tḥtāğhā؟

هيو: أحتاج إلى درجة جامعية لمدة أربع سنوات في إدارة الأعمال. بعض الخبرة السابقة في العمل ستكون مفيدة أيضًا.
hyw: ʾḥtāğ ʾlى drğẗ ğāmʿyẗ lmdʾ ẗrbʿ snwāt fy ʾdārẗ ālʾʿmāl. bʿḍ ālẖbrẗ ālsābqẗ fy ālʿml stkwn mfydʾ ẗyḍā̈.

زاك: ما نوع الخبرة التي تبحث عنها؟
zāk: mā nwʿ ālẖbrۃ ālty tbḥṯ ʿnhā؟

هيو: عمل مكتبي عام سيكون كاف. أنا لا أحتاج إلى الكثير من الخبرة. سيكون هناك تدريب على العمل للشخص المناسب.
hyw: ʿml mktby ʿām sykwn kāf. ٲnā lā ٲḥtāǧ ٳlى ālkṯyr mn ālẖbr.ۃ sykwn hnāk tdryb ʿlى ālʿml llšẖṣ ālmnāsb.

زاك: هذا رائع!
zāk: hḏā rāئʿ!

هيو: ما هي نقاط القوة لديك؟ لما ينبغي على أن أوظفك؟
hyw: mā hy nqāṭ ālqwۃ ldyk؟ lmā ynbġy ʿly ٲn ٲwẓfk؟

زاك: أنا شخص مجتهد ومتعلم سريع. أنا حريص جدًا على التعلم ولدي علاقات ممتازة مع الجميع.
zāk: ٲnā šẖṣ mǧthd wmtʿlm sryʿ. ٲnā ḥryṣ ǧdًā ʿlى āltʿlm wldy ʿlāqāt mmtāzۃ mʿ ālǧmyʿ.

هيو: جيد. ألا تمانع في العمل لساعات طويلة، أليس كذلك؟
hyw: ǧyd. ٲlā tmānʿ fy ālʿml lsāʿāt ṭwylٲ ،ۃlys kḏlk؟

زاك: لا، لا مانع على الإطلاق.
zāk: lā، lā mānʿ ʿlى ālٳṭlāq.

هيو: يمكنك التعامل مع الضغط؟
hyw: ymknk āltʿāml mʿ ālḍġṭ؟

زاك: نعم. عندما كنت أذهب إلى المدرسة، أخذت 5 دورات في كل فصل دراسي بينما كنت أعمل خمس وعشرين ساعة على الأقل كل أسبوع.
zāk: nʿm. ʿndmā knt ٲḏhb ٳlى ālmdrsٲ ،ۃẖḏt 5 dwrāt fy kl fṣl drāsy bynmā knt ٲʿml ẖms wʿšryn sāʿۃ ʿlى ālٲql kl ٲsbwʿ.

هيو: هل لديك أي أسئلة أخرى لي الآن؟
hyw: hl ldyk ٲy ٲsئlٲ ةẖrى ly ālٱn؟

زاك: لا، أعتقد أني افهم جيدًا الوظيفة.
zāk: lā، ٲʿtqd ٲny āfhm ǧydًā ālwẓyfة.

هيو: حسنًا، زاك كان من الرائع مقابلتك. شكرًا لقدومك.
hyw: ḥsnًā، zāk kān mn ālrāئʿ mqābltk. škrًā lqdwmk.

زاك: سُعدت بمقابلتك أيضًا. شكرا لك لمقابلتي.
zāk: sʿdt bmqābltk ٲyḍًā. škrā lk lmqāblty.

Job Interview

Hugh: Welcome Zach. Let's start the interview. Are you ready?

Zach: Yes, I am.

Hugh: Great. First of all, let me properly introduce myself. I am the company Logistics Manager. I need to fill an entry-level position as soon as possible.

Zach: Wonderful. Could you tell me a little bit about the position and your expectations?

Hugh: The new employee will have to work closely with the manufacturing department. There is also a requirement to deal with the bank on a daily basis.

Zach: What type of qualifications do you require?

Hugh: I require a four-year college degree in business administration. Some previous work experience would be helpful.

Zach: What kind of experience are you looking for?

Hugh: General office work is fine. I do not require a lot of experience. There will be on the job training for the right person.

Zach: That is great!

Hugh: What are your strengths? Why should I hire you?

Zach: I am a hard-working person and a fast learner. I am very eager to learn, and I get along fine with everyone.

Hugh: Alright. You do not mind working long hours, do you?

Zach: No, I do not mind at all.

Hugh: Can you handle pressure?

Zach: Yes. When I was going to school, I took 5 courses each semester while working at least twenty-five hours every week.

Hugh: Do you have any questions for me at this time?

Zach: No, I think I have a pretty good understanding of the job.

Hugh: Ok, Zach it was nice meeting you. Thank you for coming.

Zach: Nice meeting you too. Thank you for seeing me.

44. تقديم عرض – GIVING A PRESENTATION
(tqdym ʿrḍ)

سالي: سأكون مظطرة إلى تقديم عرض حول الاحتباس الحراري العالمي يوم الجمعة، وأنا متوترة جدًّا.

sāly: sˈkwn mẓṭrǃ ةاى tqdym ʿrḍ ḥwl ālāḥtbās ālḥrāry ālʿālmy ywm ālğmʿ،ة wˈnā mtwtrة ğdā.

أولغا: هناك الكثير من الأشياء التي يمكنك القيام بها لتجعلك تشعرين بمزيد من الثقة وتوتر أقل.

ˈwlġā: hnāk ālkṯyr mn ālˈšyāʾ ālty ymknk ālqyām bhā ltğʿlk tšʿryn bmzyd mn ālṯqة wtwtr ˈql.

سالي: ماذا علي أن أفعل يا أولغا؟

sāly: māḏā ʿly ˈn ˈfʿl yā ˈwlġā؟

أولغا: هل قمتِ ببحثك حول هذا الموضوع؟

ˈwlġā: hl qmt bbḥṯk ḥwl hḏā ālmwḍwʿ؟

سالي: في الحقيقة، لقد قمت بالكثير من الأبحاث حول هذا الموضوع، وأنا أعلم أنني أستطيع الإجابة عن أي أسئلة سأتلقاها من الجمهور.

sāly: fy ālḥqyq،ة lqd qmt bālkṯyr mn ālˈbḥāṯ ḥwl hḏā ālmwḍwʿ، wˈnā ˈʿlm ˈnny ˈstṭyʿ ālǃğābة ʿn ˈy ˈsئلة sˈtlqāhā mn ālğmhwr.

أولغا: تأكدي من أن يكون لديكِ مخطط لعرضك.

ˈwlġā: tˈkdy mn ˈn ykwn ldyk mḫṭṭ lʿrḍk.

سالي: صحيح معك حق. سيساعدني ذلك في تنظيم المعلومات.

sāly: ṣḥyḥ mʿk ḥq. sysāʿdny ḏlk fy tnẓym ālmʿlwmāt.

أولغا: نعم. وسوف تساعدك على معرفة ما يجب أن تقدمي أولا وثانيا وثالثا ...
ỉwlġā: nʿm. wswf tsāʿdk ʿlى mʿrfة mā yǧb ỉn tqdmy ỉwlā wṯānyā wṯālṯā ...

أولغا: فكرة جيدة! من المهم الحصول على حقائق لدعم عرضك. أنتِ تريدين أن يكون العرض ذا موثوقية.
ỉwlġā: fkrة ǧydة! mn ālmhm ālḥṣwl ʿlى ḥqāئq ldʿm ʿrḍk. ỉnt̨ trydyn ỉn ykwn ālʿrḍ ḏā mwṯwqyة.

سالي: سأفعل ذلك الآن! شكرًا لك.
sāly: sỉfʿl ḏlk ālẳn! škrًā lk.

أولغا: سوف تقومين بعرض رائع.
ỉwlġā: swf tqwmyn bʿrḍ rāئʿ.

GIVING A PRESENTATION

Sally: I will have to give a presentation on global warming on Friday, and I am so nervous.

Olga: There are a lot of things you can do to make you feel more confident and less nervous.

Sally: What should I do, Olga?

Olga: Have you done your research on the topic?

Sally: In fact, I have done a lot of research on the subject, and I know I can answer almost any questions I will receive from the audience.

Olga: Make sure to create an outline of your presentation.

Sally: You're right. This will help me organize all of the information.

Olga: Yes. It will help you figure out what should present first, second, third...

Olga: Good idea! It is important to have facts to support your presentation. You want the presentation to be credible.

Sally: I'm going to do that right now! Thank you.

Olga: You're going to have a great presentation.

45. التخرج – Graduation
(ālthrğ)

ليز: هذه باقة زهور رائعة، لمن هي؟
lyz: hdh bāqẗ zhwr rāỷʿẗ، lmn hy؟

آني: هذه الزهور لأختي سيلفيا. سوف تتخرج اليوم.
ʾny: hdh ālzhwr lʾḫty sylfyā. swf ttḫrğ ālywm.

ليز: أكيد أنها كانت مكلفة.
lyz: ʾkyd ʾnhā kānt mklfẗ

آني: لقد دفعت سبعين دولارًا.
ʾny: lqd dfʿt sbʿyn dwlārā̋.

ليز: هذا مكلف للغاية.
lyz: hdā mklf llġāyẗ.

آني: عملت أختي في السنوات الأربع الأخيرة للحصول على شهادتها. بالنسبة لي إنفاق هذا المبلغ من المال يستحق ذلك.
ʾny: ʿmlt ʾḫty fy ālsnwāt ālʾrbʿ ālʾḫyrẗ llḥṣwl ʿlى šhādthā. bālnsbẗ ly ʾnfāq hdā ālmblġ mn ālmāl ysthq dlk.

ليز: هذا لطيف جدًّا منك. أتمنى لو أننا تخرجنا اليوم. هذا رائع جدًّا!
lyz: hdā lṭyf ğdā̋ mnk. ʾtmnى lw ʾnnā tḫrğnā ālywm. hdā rāỷʿ ğdā̋!

آني: نحن لا يزال لدينا ثلاث سنوات وسنتخرج أيضًا. سنتخرج قبل أن نستوعب ذلك. الوقت يمر بسرعة حقًا.
ʾny: nḥn lā yzāl ldynā ṯlāṯ snwāt wsntḫrğ ʾyḍā̋. sntḫrğ qbl ʾn nstwʿb dlk. ālwqt ymr bsrʿẗ ḥqā̋.

GRADUATION

Liz: That is a wonderful bouquet of flowers. Who is it for?

Annie: These flowers are for my sister Silvia. She is graduating today.

Liz: It must have cost you a fortune.

Annie: I paid seventy dollars for them.

Liz: That is quite expensive.

Annie: My sister worked very the last four years for her degree. To me spending that amount of money is worth it.

Liz: That is very nice of you. I wish we were graduating today. This is so exciting!

Annie: We only have another three years and we will be done also. We'll be graduating before we realize it. Time goes by very fast.

46. الهالوين – HALLOWEEN
(ālhālwyn)

ايلي: أليسون, هل تصدقين أن الهالوين غدًا؟ الوقت يمر بسرعة! اليوم هو 30 أكتوبر! هل قررت بالفعل ما هو الزي الذي سوف ترتدينه؟

āyly: ỉlyswn› hl tṣdqyn ỉn ālhālwyn ġdًā؟ ālwqt ymr bsrʿة! ālywm hw 30 ỉktwbr! hl qrrt bālfʿl mā hw ālzy āldy swf trtdynh؟

أليسون: لم أقرر بعد فأنا مترددة كثيرًا. أريد ارتداء إما زي خبزة محمصة أو زي مغني راب. لطالما تساءلت عن سبب تقاليد التنكر في الهالوين.

ỉlyswn: lm ỉqrr bʿd fỉnā mtrddة ktyrًā. ỉryd ārtdāʾ ỉmā zy ẖbzة mḥmṣỉ ةw zy mġny rāb. lṭālmā tsāʾlt ʿn sbb tqālyd āltnkr fy ālhālwyn.

ايلي: التنكر يجعل الاحتفال بالعيد أكثر متعة!

āyly: āltnkr yǧʿl ālāḥtfāl bālʿyd ỉktr mtʿة!

أليسون: نعم، أتذكر أنني استمتعت كثيرًا في العام الماضي عندما أخذتني أمي في زي قطة. هل تعرف ماذا تريد أن تكون يا ايلي؟

ỉlyswn: nʿm، ỉtdkr ỉnny āstmtʿt ktyrًā fy ālʿām ālmāḍy ʿndmā ỉẖdtny ỉmy fy zy qṭ.ة hl tʿrf mādā tryd ỉn tkwn yā āyly؟

ايلي: أريد أن أتنكر في زي سنجاب!

āyly: ỉryd ỉn ỉtnkr fy zy snǧāb!

أليسون: فكرة رائعة!

ỉlyswn: fkrة rāئʿة!

ايلي: جيد! إذًا سوف تكونين مغنية راب العصابات وسأكون أنا سنجاب. لِنذهب ونسأل أمي إذا كان بإمكاننا أن نذهب للقيام بلعبة خدعة أم حلوى ليلة الغد.

āyly: ğyd! ịḏā̃ swf tkwnyn mġnyẗ rāb ālʿṣābāt wsỉkwn ỉnā snğāb. lnḏhb wnsỉl ỉmy ịḏā kān bịmkānnā ỉn nḏhb llqyām blʿbẗ ẖdʿẗ ỉm ḥlwى lylẗ ālġd.

أليسون: حسنًا، لِنذهب ونسأل أمي!

ỉlyswn: ḥsnā̃، lnḏhb wnsỉl ỉmy!

HALLOWEEN

Eli: Can you believe that tomorrow is Halloween Allison? Time goes by so fast! Today is October 30th! Have you already decided what costume you want to wear?

Allison: I'm still undecided. I want to wear either a toaster costume or a gangster rapper costume. I have always wondered why it's a tradition to dress up for Halloween.

Eli: Dressing up makes celebrating the holiday much more fun!

Allison: Yes, I remember having a lot of fun last year when mom took me around in a cat outfit. Do you know what you want to be yet, Eli?

Eli: I want to a chipmunk!

Allison: That's a great idea!

Eli: Great! So you will be a gangster rapper and I will be a chipmunk. Let's go ask mom if we can go trick-or-treating tomorrow night by ourselves.

Allison: Ok, let's go ask mom!

47. في فندق - AT A HOTEL
(fy fndq)

موظف استقبال الفندق: مساء الخير.

mwẓf āstqbāl ālfndq: msā' ālẖyr.

ايلي: مرحبًا، مساء الخير. أنا وزوجتي بحاجة إلى غرفة لليلة من فضلك. هل لديك واحدة متاحة بالصدفة؟

āyly: mrḥbā، msā' ālẖyr. ỉnā wzwǧty bḥāǧ̈ ỉlى ġrfẗ llylẗ mn fḍlk. hl ldyk wāḥdẗ mtāḥẗ bālṣdfẗ؟

موظف استقبال الفندق: هل لديك حجز؟

mwẓf āstqbāl ālfndq: hl ldyk ḥǧz؟

ايلي: لسوء الحظ، ليس لدينا حجز.

āyly: lsw' ālḥẓ، lys ldynā ḥǧz.

موظف استقبال الفندق: حسنًا. اسمح لي أن اتحقق وأرى ما لدينا. يبدو أنك محظوظ. لدينا غرفة واحدة فقط.

mwẓf āstqbāl ālfndq: ḥsnā. āsmḥ ly ỉn ātḥqq wỉrى mā ldynā. ybdw ỉnk mḥẓwẓ. ldynā ġrfẗ wāḥdẗ fqṭ.

ايلي: ممتاز. كنا نتجول طوال اليوم ونحن متعبان جدًا. نحتاج فقط إلى مكان للاسترخاء لبقية الليل.

āyly: mmtāz. knā ntǧwl ṭwāl ālywm wnḥn mtʿbān ǧdā. nḥtāǧ fqṭ ỉlى mkān llāstrẖā' lbqyẗ āllyl.

موظف استقبال الفندق: هذه الغرفة ستفيدك. إنها غرفة مريحة مع سرير بحجم كبير ومطبخ كامل.
mwẓf āstqbāl ālfndq: hḏh ālġrfẗ stfydk. ỉnhā ġrfẗ mryḥẗ mʿ sryr bḥǧm kbyr wmṭbḫ kāml.

ايلي: كم هو سعر الليلة؟
āyly: km hw sʿr āllylẗ؟

موظف استقبال الفندق: 179 دولارًا للغرفة. هل هناك شخص آخر سيقيم معكما في الغرفة؟
mwẓf āstqbāl ālfndq: 179 dwlārā̃ llġrf.ẗ hl hnāk šḫṣ ʾāḫr syqym mʿkmā fy ālġrfẗ؟

ايلي: لا نحن فقط اثنان. أعلم أنه وقت متأخر من الليل، ولكن هل هناك مطعم مفتوح في مكان قريب؟
āyly: lā nḥn fqṭ āṯnān. ỉʿlm ỉnh wqt mtỉḫr mn āllyl، wlkn hl hnāk mṭʿm mftwḥ fy mkān qryb؟

موظف استقبال الفندق: يوجد مطعم مفتوح لساعة أخرى في الفندق. هل ترغب في دفع ثمن الغرفة ببطاقة ائتمان؟
mwẓf āstqbāl ālfndq: ywǧd mṭʿm mftwḥ lsāʿỉ ẗḫrى fy ālfndq. hl trġb fy dfʿ ṯmn ālġrfẗ bbṭāqẗ āئtmān؟

ايلي: نعم، تفضل.
āyly: nʿm، tfḍl.

موظف استقبال الفندق: شكرًا لك. كل شيء على ما يرام. استمتع ببقية الليل.
mwẓf āstqbāl ālfndq: škrā̃ lk. kl šyʾ ʿlى mā yrām. āstmtʿ bbqyẗ āllyl.

At a Hotel

Hotel Receptionist: Good evening.

Eli: Hello, good evening. My wife and I need a room for the night please. By chance do you have one available?

Hotel Receptionist: Do you have a reservation?

Eli: Unfortunately, we do not have a reservation.

Hotel Receptionist: Ok. Let me check and see what we have. It looks you're in luck. We have only one room left.

Eli: Excellent. We have been driving all day and we're very tired. We just need a place to relax for the rest of the night.

Hotel Receptionist: This room should do just fine then. It is a cozy room with a king size bed and full kitchen.

Eli: How much is it for the night?

Hotel Receptionist: It's $179 for the room. Is there anyone else staying in the room with you?

Eli: It's just the two of us. I know that it's late at night, but is there any restaurant open nearby?

Hotel Receptionist: There's a restaurant open for another hour in the hotel. Do you want to pay for the room with a credit card?

Eli: Yes. Here you go.

Hotel Receptionist: Thank you. You're all set. Enjoy the rest of the night.

48. طالبة أجنبية – A Foreign Student
(ṭālbᶦ ᶦ̈ǧnbyᶦ̈)

درو: مرحبًا، هل أنتِ السيدة مكنمارا؟
drw: mrḥbā̈، hl ᶦnt ālsydᶦ̈ mknmārā؟

السيدة مكنمارا: نعم، أنا كذلك. يجب أن تكوني درو. كنا نتوقع منك القدوم.
ālsydᶦ̈ mknmārā: nʿm، ᶦnā kḏlk. yǧb ᶦn tkwny drw. knā ntwqʿ mnk ālqdwm .

درو: كان من المفترض أن آتي قبل يومين، لكن سفرتي من كولومبيا تأخرت.
drw: kān mn ālmftrḍ ᶦn ᶦ̄ty qbl ywmyn، lkn sfrty mn kwlwmbyā tᶦḫrt.

السيدة مكنمارا: حسنًا، يسرني أنك نجحت في تحقيق ذلك بأمان، وهذا هو الأهم. هل تريدين بعض الشاي؟
ālsydᶦ̈ mknmārā: ḥsnā̈، ysrny ᶦnk nǧḥt fy tḥqyq ḏlk bᶦmān، whḏā hw ālᶦhm. hl trydyn bʿḍ ālšāy؟

درو: نعم من فضلك، إذا لم يكن هناك الكثير من المتاعب. لديكِ منزل جميل.
drw: nʿm mn fḍlk، !ḏā lm ykn hnāk ālkṯyr mn ālmtāʿb. ldyk mnzl ǧmyl.

السيدة مكنمارا: شكرًا. انتقلنا إلى كاليفورنيا من كولومبيا قبل خمس سنوات وقررت شراء هذا المنزل. نحن نحب ذلك تمامًا.
ālsydᶦ̈ mknmārā: škrā̈. āntqlnā !lى kālyfwrnyā mn kwlwmbyā qbl ḫms snwāt wqrrt šrāʾ hḏā ālmnzl. nḥn nḥb ḏlk tmāmā̈.

درو: أحضرت لك هدية.
drw: ᶦḥḍrt lk hdyᶦ̈.

السيدة مكنمارا: لا لم يكن من الضروري. إنها قلادة جميلة. شكرًا لك. إلى متى سوف تبقين هنا؟

ālsydẗ mknmārā: lā lm ykn mn ālḍrwry. ̧nhā qlādẗ ğmyl.ẗ škrā̃ lk. ̧lى mtى swf tbqyn hnā؟

درو: مرحبًا بك. أخطط للبقاء في كاليفورنيا لمدة خمسة أشهر لممارسة اللغة الإنجليزية. أنا متحمس حقًا للذهاب إلى المدرسة الإنجليزية والتعلم.

drw: mrḥbā̃ bk. ʾẖṭṭ llbqāʾ fy kālyfwrnyā lmdẗ ẖmsʾ ẗšhr lmmārsẗ āllġẗ āļnğlyzyʾ .ẗnā mtḥms ḥqā̃ llḏhāb ̧lى ālmdrsẗ āļnğlyzyẗ wāltʿlm.

السيدة مكنمارا: جيد، سأريكِ غرفتك حيث يمكنكِ الاسترخاء. لا بد أنك مرهقة من السفر.

ālsydẗ mknmārā: ğyd، sʾryk ġrftk ḥyṯ ymknk ālāstrẖāʾ. lā bd ʾnk mrhqẗ mn ālsfr.

A Foreign Student

Drew: Hello, are you Mrs. McNamara?

Mrs. McNamara: Yes, I am. You must be Drew. We have been expecting you.

Drew: I was supposed to arrive two days ago, but my flight out of Colombia was delayed.

Mrs. McNamara: Well, I'm glad that you made it safely, that's is what is most important. Would you like some tea?

Drew: I would love some, if it's not too much trouble. You have a beautiful home.

Mrs. McNamara: Thank you. We moved to California from Colombia five years ago and decided to buy this house. We absolutely love it.

Drew: I brought you a gift.

Mrs. McNamara: Oh, you shouldn't have. This is a beautiful necklace. Thank you. How long will you be here for?

Drew: You're welcome. I plan to stay in California for five months to practice speaking English. I am really excited to go to the English school and learn.

Mrs. McNamara: Well, let me show you your room and you can relax. You must be tired from all of the traveling.

49. مماطلة – PROCRASTINATION
(mmāṭlẗ)

سكوتي: هل كتبت تقريرك البحثي أم لا؟ سينتهي الموعد في غضون أسبوعين.
skwty: hl ktbt tqryrk ālbḥṯy ꞌm lā؟ synthy ālmwʿd fy ġḍwn ꞌsbwʿyn.

ميريديث: لا، لم أبدأ العمل عليه بعد. لدي متسع من الوقت للقيام بذلك في الأسبوع المقبل.
myrydyṯ: lā، lm ꞌbdꞌ ālʿml ʿlyh bʿd. ldy mtsʿ mn ālwqt llqyām bḏlk fy ālꞌsbwʿ ālmqbl.

سكوتي: تذكري هذا ما قلتيه الأسبوع الماضي والأسبوع الذي سبقه. لديكِ الكثير من وقت الفراغ خلال العطلة، يجب عليكِ أن تنجزيه.
skwty: tḏkry hḏā mā qltyh ālꞌsbwʿ ālmāḍy wālꞌsbwʿ ālḏy sbqh. ldyk ālkṯyr mn wqt ālfrāġ ẖlāl ālʿṭlẗ، yǧb ʿlyk ꞌn tnǧzyh.

ميريديث: المشكلة هي أنني أواجه صعوبة في ذلك الفصل وأعتقد أنني قد أحتاج إلى الحصول على مدرس. وإلا فقد أرسب في الفصل بالكامل.
myrydyṯ: ālmšklẗ hy ꞌnny ꞌwāǧh ṣʿwbẗ fy ḏlk ālfṣl wꞌʿtqd ꞌnny qd ꞌḥtāǧ ꞌlى ālḥṣwl ʿlى mdrs. wꞌlā fqd ꞌrsb fy ālfṣl bālkāml.

سكوتي: لدي حل. توقفي عن التفكير في الحصول على المساعدة واحصلي على مدرس.
skwty: ldy ḥl. twqfy ʿn āltfkyr fy ālḥṣwl ʿlى ālmsāʿdẗ wāḥṣly ʿlى mdrs.

ميريديث: أنتِ على حق. أحتاج لأن أكون نشيطة وأحصل على مساعدة. سوف أبدأ بالبحث غداً.
myrydyṯ: ꞌnt ʿlى ḥq. ꞌḥtāǧ lꞌn ꞌkwn nšyṭẗ wꞌḥṣl ʿlى msāʿdẗ.swf ꞌbdꞌ bālbḥṯ ġdًā.

سكوتي: غدًا؟ لا, عليك أن تجدي واحدًا اليوم!
skwty: ġdā̃؟ lā, ʿlyk ˀn tğdy wāḥdā̃ ālywm!

ميريديث: أعلم، أنا أمزح. سأفعلها اليوم.
myrydyṯ: ˀʿlm، ˀnā ˀmzḥ. sˀfʿlhā ālywm.

PROCRASTINATION

Scottie: Have you written your research report yet? It's due in two weeks.

Meredith: No, I haven't started working on it yet. I have plenty of time to do it next week though.

Scottie: I distinctly remember that's what you said last week and the week before that. Since you have so much free time during the holiday you should get it done.

Meredith: The problem is that I am struggling in that class and I think I might need to get a tutor. Otherwise I might fail the entire class.

Scottie: I have a solution. Stop thinking about getting help and get a tutor.

Meredith: You're right. I need to be proactive and get help. I will start looking tomorrow.

Scottie: Tomorrow? No, you have to find one today!

Meredith: I know, I'm just kidding. I will do it today.

50. أين هو أخي – WHERE'S MY BROTHER
(ˀyn hw ˀẖy)

كاريسا: لم أستطع العثور على أخي الصغير دانيال. اعتقدت أنه كان ورائي والآن هو مفقود. من فضلك ساعدني.
kārysā: lm ˀstṭʿ ālʿṯwr ʿlˀ ىẖy ālṣġyr dānyāl. āʿtqdt ˀnh kān wrāئy wālˀn hw mfqwd. mn fḍlk sāʿdny.

ضابط شرطة: ربما ضاع في الحشد. هناك الكثير من الناس يتسوقون للعطلة. ماذا يرتدي؟
ḍābṭ šrṭ:ة rbmā ḍāʿ fy ālḥšd. hnāk ālkṯyr mn ālnās ytswqwn llʿṭl.ة māḏā yrtdy؟

كاريسا: يرتدي سترة زرقاء وشورت أسود. عمره 5 سنوات فحسب.
kārysā: yrtdy strة zrqāʾ wšwrt ˀswd. ʿmrh 5 snwāt fḥsb.

ضابط الشرطة: أعتقد أنني رأيته يدخل غرفة ارتداء الملابس. سأتحقق. هل شعره أشقر؟
ḍābṭ ālšrṭˀ :ةʿtqd ˀnny rˀyth ydẖl ġrfة ārtdāʾ ālmlābs. sˀtḥqq. hl šʿrh ˀšqr؟

كاريسا: نعم. هل وجدته؟
kārysā: nʿm. hl wǧdth؟

ضابط الشرطة: لا، لم يكن هو. دعينا نتحقق من متجر الألعاب المجاور.
ḍābṭ ālšrṭ:ة lā، lm ykn hw. dʿynā ntḥqq mn mtǧr ālˀlʿāb ālmǧāwr.

كاريسا: يحب اللعب بالمركبات، كان يجب أن أفكر في ذلك!
kārysā: yḥb āllʿb bālmrkbāt، kān yǧb ˀn ˀfkr fy ḏlk!

ضابط الشرطة: أرى الكثير من الأطفال في كل مكان. هل أي منهم هو أخوك؟
ḍābṭ ālšrṭۃ: ʾrى ālktyr mn ālʾṭfāl fy kl mkān. hl ʾy mnhm hw ʾẖwk؟

كاريسا: دانيال! ها أنت ذا، لا تتجول هكذا مرة أخرى! لقد أخفتني بشدة!
kārysā: dānyāl! hā ʾnt ḏā، lā ttǧwl hkḏā mrʾ ۃẖrى! lqd ʾẖftny bšdۃ!

ضابط الشرطة: الرجاء مراقبته حتى لا يحدث ذلك مرة أخرى. يمكن أن يكون تجوله وحده خطرًا.
ḍābṭ ālšrṭ:ۃ ālrǧāʾ mrāqbth ḥtى lā yḥdṯ ḏlk mrʾ ۃẖr.ى ymkn ʾn ykwn tǧwlh wḥdh ẖṭrā̈.

كاريسا: أنت على حق. سأحرص على مراقبته.
kārysā: ʾnt ʿlى ḥq. sʾḥrṣ ʿlى mrāqbth.

ضابط الشرطة: جيد. اذهبي الآن والتحقي بوالديك واحصلا على يوم رائع.
ḍābṭ ālšrṭ:ۃ ǧyd. āḏhby ālʾn wālthqy bwāldyk wāḥṣlā ʿlى ywm rāئʿ.

كاريسا: شكرًا لك أيها الضابط على مساعدتك.
kārysā: škrā̈ lk ʾyhā ālḍābṭ ʿlى msāʿdtk.

WHERE'S MY BROTHER

Carissa: I can't find my little brother, Daniel. I thought he was right behind me and now he's missing. Please help me.

Police officer: He probably got lost in the crowd. There are a lot of people shopping for the holidays. What kind of clothes is he wearing?

Carissa: He has a blue jacket and black shorts. He's only 5 years old.

Police officer: I think I saw him go into the dressing room. Let me check. Does he have blonde hair?

Carissa: Yes. Did you find him?

Police officer: No, that was not him. Let's check the toy store next door.

Carissa: He loves playing with Legos, I should have thought of that!

Police officer: I see a lot of children everywhere. Are any of them your brother?

Carissa: Daniel! There you are, don't you wander off like that again! You scared me to death!

Police officer: Please keep an eye on him so that this doesn't happen again. It can be dangerous wandering around all by himself.

Carissa: You're right. I will take better care of watching him.

Police officer: Alright. Now go find your parents and have a good day.

Carissa: Thank you officer for all of your help.

Conclusion

Well reader, we hope that you found these dual language dialogues helpful. Remember that the best way to learn this material is through repetition, memorization and conversation.

We encourage you to review the dialogues again, find a friend and practice your Arabic by role playing. Not only will you have more fun doing it this way, but you will find that you will remember even more!

Keep in mind, that every day you practice, the closer you will get to speaking fluently.

You can expect many more books from us, so keep your eyes peeled. Thank you again for reading our book and we look forward to seeing you again.

About the Author

Touri is an innovative language education brand that is disrupting the way we learn languages. Touri has a mission to make sure language learning is not just easier but engaging and a ton of fun

Besides the excellent books that they create, Touri also has an active website, which offers live fun and immersive 1-on-1 online language lessons with native instructors at nearly anytime of the day.

Additionally, Touri provides the best tips to improving your memory retention, confidence while speaking and fast track your progress on your journey to fluency.

Check out https://touri.co for more information.

ONE LAST THING...

If you enjoyed this book or found it useful, we would be very grateful if you posted a short review.

Your support really does make a difference and we read all the reviews personally. Your feedback will make this book even better.

Thanks again for your support!

www.ingramcontent.com/pod-product-compliance
Lightning Source LLC
Chambersburg PA
CBHW072020110526
44592CB00012B/1379
9781953149220